KT-513-221

Im   e Your Bridge

Teach®
Yourself

Improve Your Bridge
David Bird

For UK order enquiries: please contact Bookpoint Ltd,
130 Milton Park, Abingdon, Oxon OX14 4SB.
Telephone: +44 (0) 1235 827720. Fax: +44 (0) 1235 400454.
Lines are open 09.00–17.00, Monday to Saturday, with a 24-hour
message answering service. Details about our titles and how to
order are available at www.teachyourself.com

For USA order enquiries: please contact McGraw-Hill Customer
Services, PO Box 545, Blacklick, OH 43004-0545, USA.
Telephone: 1-800-722-4726. Fax: 1-614-755-5645.

For Canada order enquiries: please contact McGraw-Hill Ryerson
Ltd, 300 Water St, Whitby, Ontario L1N 9B6, Canada.
Telephone: 905 430 5000. Fax: 905 430 5020.

Long renowned as the authoritative source for self-guided learning –
with more than 50 million copies sold worldwide – the **Teach Yourself**
series includes over 500 titles in the fields of languages, crafts, hobbies,
business, computing and education.

British Library Cataloguing in Publication Data: a catalogue record
for this title is available from the British Library.

Library of Congress Catalog Card Number: on file.

First published in UK 2006 by Hodder Education, part of
Hachette UK, 338 Euston Road, London NW1 3BH.

First published in US 2006 by The McGraw-Hill Companies, Inc.

This edition published 2010.

Previously published as *Teach Yourself Better Bridge*.

The **Teach Yourself** name is a registered trade mark of
Hodder Headline.

Copyright © 2006, 2010 David Bird

Typeset by MPS Limited, a Macmillan Company.

Printed in Great Britain for Hodder Education, an Hachette UK
Company, 338 Euston Road, London NW1 3BH, by CPI Cox &
Wyman, Reading, Berkshire RG1 8EX.

The publisher has used its best endeavours to ensure that the URLs
for external websites referred to in this book are correct and active
at the time of going to press. However, the publisher and the
author have no responsibility for the websites and can make no
guarantee that a site will remain live or that the content will remain
relevant, decent or appropriate.

Hachette UK's policy is to use papers that are natural, renewable
and recyclable products and made from wood grown in sustainable
forests. The logging and manufacturing processes are expected to
conform to the environmental regulations of the country of origin.

Impression number   10 9 8 7 6 5 4 3 2 1

Year   2014 2013 2012 2011 2010

Contents

Meet the author

Welcome to *Improve Your Bridge*!

The accompanying volume, *Win at Bridge*, covered the basics of
the game. All the opening bids were described and how you should
respond to them. There were further chapters on the opener's
rebid and responder's rebid. In the section on slam bidding, the
cue-bidding of controls and basic Blackwood were covered. The
two chapters on defensive bidding addressed take-out and penalty
doubles, also the various types of overcall and how to respond
to them. The sections on dummy play described some of the
techniques required for both suit and no-trump contracts. The basic
moves in defence, including opening leads and signals, were also
covered.

So, what areas will be tackled in this new book, *Improve Your Bridge*?
We will look at the most popular bidding conventions used in
tournament bridge, where players strive to the utmost to bid their
own cards accurately and to disrupt the opponents' auction. We will
see many of the most important ways to play the dummy, including
elimination play, the cross-ruff, dummy reversal, communications
play, safety plays and counting the hand. Finally, we will look more
closely at defence, in particular at communications, promoting
trump tricks and holding up high cards. Absorb all the advice and
you will achieve every bridge fanatic's aim – to become a better
player. Good luck!

David Bird

Only got a minute?

The accompanying volume, *Win at Bridge,* covers the basics of the game. It explains opening bids and responses, the rebids by opener and responder, and how to judge when to bid a game or a slam. The basic techniques of dummy play and defence are covered too, along with the scoring.

Improve Your Bridge moves up a level. It describes the most popular conventions used in duplicate bridge, such as transfer responses to 1NT and 2NT, weak two-bids, Roman Key-card Blackwood, negative doubles, responsive doubles and competitive doubles, also two-suited overcalls. It explains several important ways of playing the dummy, such as elimination play, dummy reversal, cross-ruffing and avoidance play. You will discover how to benefit from safety plays, counting the hand and clues from the bidding. The many ways of creating and destroying communications are described, both for declarer and the defenders. The important techniques for promoting trump tricks in defence are explained. Finally, the mechanics of duplicate bridge are covered, so you will know what to expect if you decide to venture into the exciting world of tournament bridge.

5 Only got five minutes?

The accompanying volume, *Win at Bridge*, covers the basics of the game. It explains opening bids and responses, the rebids by opener and responder, and how to judge when to bid a game or a slam. The basic techniques of dummy play and defence are covered too, along with the scoring. *Improve Your Bridge* moves up one level, describing the most popular conventions used in duplicate bridge, various techniques available to the declarer and how the defenders can combine together to beat the contract.

The bidding methods described include Roman Key-card Blackwood, weak two-bids, negative doubles and responsive doubles. Two suited overcalls are described: the Unusual No-trump and Michaels cue-bids. The book explains also the many uses of a bid in the opponents' suit.

Some styles of declarer play remain unknown to those who have never read about them. The book describes reversing the dummy, where declarer takes several ruffs in his own hand. It covers also elimination play, where you remove a defender's safe exit cards and then throw him on lead to give you an extra trick. It describes how you can benefit, both as declarer and as a defender, from counting. You can count points, distribution and tricks. In particular, declarer can take two-way finesses against a missing queen with a high rate of success. By counting the defenders' lengths in spades, hearts and clubs, for example, you may discover that East has four diamonds and West has two. East will then be the favourite to hold the missing ♦Q.

Many plays are concerned with communications. Declarer can preserve his communications with the dummy by winning the opening lead in the right hand or by winning the first trick with a higher card than is necessary. The defenders can preserve their communications by holding up a high card on the first or second round, so it can be used as an entry later. Just as important is the attack on the opponents' communications. Declarer achieves this most easily with the hold-up play. Similarly, the defenders must try to break declarer's communications with the dummy. To do this effectively, they must use count signals and these are clearly explained.

The final chapter of the book covers the mechanics of duplicate bridge. The scoring on each board is explained, how the pairs move from table to table and how the winners will eventually be determined. Duplicate bridge, usually in a club, is the competitive form of the game. When you play rubber bridge or Chicago, you can do well in a session merely because you picked up some good cards. In duplicate bridge each hand is played more than once, so you can compare your result with those of other competitors who hold exactly the same cards. The luck factor is removed, to a large extent, and skill prevails!

10 Only got ten minutes?

The accompanying volume, *Win at Bridge*, covers the basics of the game. It explains opening bids and responses, the rebids by opener and responder, and how to judge when to bid a game or a slam. The basic techniques of dummy play and defence are covered too. *Improve Your Bridge* moves up a level. It describes the most popular conventions in duplicate bridge, several techniques available to the declarer and how the defenders can combine together to beat the contract.

The bidding methods described include Roman Key-card Blackwood. In the basic form of Blackwood, the first response defined merely how many aces are held. RKCB, as it is called, enquires also about the king and queen of trumps, which are equally important cards. You can discover exactly which side-suit kings partner holds, too. Nearly all duplicate players use this excellent method. Three types of conventional double are explained: negative, responsive and competitive doubles. In rubber bridge, it is normal to play that a double of an overcall (for example, 2♦ bid over an opponent's 1♠) is for penalties. Most duplicate players prefer to use negative doubles, where a double of an overcall is for take-out. A responsive double arises when partner doubles and the third player raises (an auction such as 1♥ – Dble – 2♥ – Dble). Again such a double is for take-out. A competitive double occurs when partner's overcall is followed by a raise (1♦ – 1♥ – 2♦ – Dble). Such a double will show both the unbid suits and some tolerance, usually a doubleton, for partner's suit.

In social bridge, opening bids such as 2♠ and 2♥ have traditionally been played as strong. In the tournament world, most players use these openings to show a weak hand with a six-card suit and around 5-9 points. The objective is to disrupt the opponent's auction as well as to describe your hand to partner. These openings and the appropriate responses are described. When partner has opened or overcalled, you will want to raise pre-emptively when you hold a relatively weak hand and four-card or longer support. To allow you to do this, while still being able to show a genuine raise, you must make use of bids in the opponent's suit. For example, 1♠ – 2♦ – 3♠ (where 2♦ is an overcall) shows a weak hand with good spade support; 1♠ – 2♦ – 3♦ shows at least a genuine limit raise. Similarly, a cue-bid in the opponent's suit shows a strong hand when responding to a take-out double. Two suited overcalls are described. The Unusual No-trump (for example, a 2NT overcall of 1♠) shows at least five cards in each of the minor suits. A Michaels cue-bid shows a two-suiter including any unbid major suits. So, an overcall of 2♦ over 1♦ shows both major suits. An overcall of 2♥ over 1♥ shows five spades and five cards in one of the minors.

Moving to declarer play, the idea of reversing the dummy is explained. Suppose you have five trumps in your hand and three in the dummy. Scoring a ruff in the hand with three trumps will increase your trump tricks from five to six. Taking a ruff in the hand with five trumps will not increase your total. Suppose, however, that you take three ruffs in the long-trump hand. Now you will score three trump tricks in dummy and three ruffs, a total of six! This is the idea behind a dummy reversal. The book also describes elimination play, where you remove a defender's safe exit cards and then throw him on lead to give you an extra trick. Suppose you have a side suit of ♣A 8 2 opposite ♣K 7. By cashing the two top cards and ruffing the third round, you can 'eliminate clubs'. A defender will not then be able to lead a club without giving you a ruff-and-discard. After eliminating two suits, you can throw a defender on lead and force him to lead the third suit to your advantage. Opportunities for elimination play arise very frequently.

The book describes how you can benefit from counting, both as declarer and as a defender. You can count points, distribution and tricks. Suppose a defender declined to open the bidding and has already shown up with 10 points. Since he did not open, you can place the remaining honour cards with his partner and play accordingly. Counting distribution (suit lengths) will allow you to take two-way finesses against a missing queen with a high rate of success. Suppose you count the defenders' length in spades, hearts and clubs, for example, finding that East has four diamonds and West has two. East will then be favourite to hold the missing ♦Q and you will finesse accordingly.

Many plays are concerned with communications. Declarer can preserve his communications by winning the opening lead in the right hand or by winning the first trick with a higher card than is necessary. For example, with ♠Q 7 2 in the dummy and ♠A 10 2 in your hand you may choose to win a spade lead with the ace, rather than the 10. You can then reach dummy with the ♠Q later. The defenders can preserve their communications by holding up a high card on the first or second round; it can then be used as a subsequent entry. Just as important is the attack on the opponents' communications. Declarer achieves this most easily with the hold-up play. To break declarer's communications with the dummy, the defenders must use count signals (a high card with an even number of cards, low with an odd number).

The final chapter of the book covers the mechanics of duplicate bridge. The book explains the scoring of each board, how the pairs move from table to table and how the winners are eventually determined. Duplicate bridge, usually in a club, is the competitive form of the game. When you play rubber bridge or Chicago, you can do well in a session merely because you picked up some good cards. In duplicate bridge each hand is played more than once and your results are compared with those of other competitors who hold exactly the same cards. Suppose you go one down in 4♠ at rubber bridge. You can mutter 'that was unlucky' and move to the next deal. In a duplicate tournament, you may find that most of the other declarers made it! By discovering how they succeeded, you will greatly improve your game.

1

Preserving declarer's communications

In this chapter you will learn:
- *how to duck to preserve an entry to dummy*
- *how to duck to guard against a bad break*
- *how to duck twice in a suit*
- *how to use the trump suit for entries*
- *how to win the opening lead in the right hand.*

Nothing is more disheartening than to see winners in the dummy but to have no way to reach them. In this chapter we will look at the most important techniques to help you stay in touch with the dummy.

Ducking to preserve an honour as an entry

When you are setting up dummy's long suit in a no-trump contract, it is often beneficial to duck an early round. By doing so, you preserve dummy's honour(s) as a means of entering the dummy later.

Look at the diamond suit on this deal:

♠ A
♥ 5 4
♦ A K 9 7 5 2
♣ J 7 6 4

♠ Q J 10 6 4
♥ Q 9
♦ J 10 6
♣ Q 8 2

♠ 8 5 3 2
♥ K 10 7
♦ Q 4
♣ K 9 5 3

♠ K 9 7
♥ A J 8 6 3 2
♦ 8 3
♣ A 10

West	North	East	South
–	–	–	1♥
Pass	2♦	Pass	2♥
Pass	3♣	Pass	3NT
End			

West leads the ♠Q against 3NT. How can you make nine tricks?

You have six tricks on top and must seek three more tricks from one of the red suits. Setting up the hearts is no good because you would probably have to give up two tricks in the process and would then lose two hearts and three spades. You would 'lose the race'.

A better idea is to establish dummy's diamonds. Provided the defenders' cards in the suit divide 3–2, you can set up the three extra winners you need by surrendering the lead just once. How should the play go?

Suppose you play the ace and king of diamonds, both defenders following, and then lead a third round of diamonds to West's jack. You will have three diamond winners in dummy, yes, but they will be stranded. There will be no way to reach them. A better idea is to lead a low diamond from dummy at Trick 2, allowing the defenders to win the first round of the suit. Do you see the point of this? When you regain the lead you can cross to the ♦A, cash the ♦K and score five diamond tricks. In other words, you will have an entry to the diamond winners in dummy.

Ducking to guard against a bad break

On the last deal it was clear that you would have to lose a round of diamonds, even if the defenders' cards divided 3–2, the most favourable break possible. Sometimes you duck an early round of dummy's long suit, just in case it breaks badly. Look at this deal:

```
            ♠ 8 7 5
            ♥ 6 3
            ♦ 9 6
            ♣ A K Q 8 7 2
♠ K J 3          N          ♠ Q 9 4
♥ Q 9 7 4                   ♥ K 8 2
♦ Q J 10 5 2  W     E       ♦ 8 7 3
♣ 9              S          ♣ J 10 5 3
            ♠ A 10 6 2
            ♥ A J 10 5
            ♦ A K 4
            ♣ 6 4
```

West	North	East	South
–	–	–	1NT (15–17)
Pass	3NT	End	

West leads the ♦Q against 3NT. You have seven top tricks and need two more tricks to make the contract. If the defenders' clubs break 3–2, you can simply play the suit from the top (beginning with the ace, king and queen). The remaining three cards will then be good and you will score an overtrick.

What will happen if you follow this line and the defenders' clubs break 4–1, as in the diagram? You will go down! You could establish two extra winners in clubs, by giving up a club trick, but you would have no way to reach them. Since you need only five club tricks to bring your total to nine, you should duck the first round of clubs. In other words, after winning the diamond lead you play a low club from both hands.

You win the defenders' return and cross to dummy with a club to the ace. The king and queen will draw East's remaining clubs and the ♣8–7 will bring your total to nine tricks. This is an example of a 'safety play', a play that you make to guard against a bad break in a suit. If clubs had broken 3–2, the safety play would have cost you an overtrick, since you would make five club tricks instead of the six that were available. However, this is a small premium to pay to ensure that you make the contract whenever the clubs are 4–1.

Insight: Safety plays in a pairs

In a duplicate pairs a score difference of 20 or 30 (for an overtrick) represents total victory against another pair playing the same contract. The safety play of ducking a club would not therefore be attractive in a pairs. You would lose out on the 68% of deals where clubs broke 3–2 and an overtrick was available.

Ducking twice in a suit

Sometimes you have to duck twice in a suit, preserving dummy's ace as an entry on the third round. Look at the diamond suit on the next deal:

```
                    ♠ 8 7 5
                    ♥ 6 3
                    ♦ A 10 7 6 2
                    ♣ 9 7 3
    ♠ Q 10 6 2         N          ♠ J 9 3
    ♥ J 8 2      W          E     ♥ Q 9 7 5
    ♦ Q 4                         ♦ K J 8
    ♣ J 6 5 2           S         ♣ Q 10 4
                    ♠ A K 4
                    ♥ A K 10 4
                    ♦ 9 5 3
                    ♣ A K 8
```

West	North	East	South
–	–	–	2NT
Pass	3NT	End	

West leads the ♠2 against 3NT. You can count seven top winners and will need to establish two more tricks from dummy's diamond suit. This can be done, provided the defenders' diamonds divide 3-2, but you will need an entry to dummy to reach the two long diamonds. The entry can only be the ♦A, so you must play low on the first two rounds of the suit. How does the play go?

You win East's ♠J with the ♠A and play a low diamond from both hands. East wins the diamond trick and returns another spade. You win with the ♠K and, once again, play a low diamond from both hands. The defenders win the trick and cash two spade tricks. (You knew they would have only two spades to cash because West's fourth-best lead of the ♠2 showed that he held a four-card suit.) When you regain the lead, you cross to the ♦A on the third round of the suit. The lead will then be in dummy – just where you want it! You cash the 10 and 7 of diamonds and that brings your total to nine.

Using the trump suit for entries

The contracts we have seen so far have all been played in no-trumps. Playing with a trump suit may affect matters in two ways: you can establish a side suit by taking ruffs in that suit; you can also use the trump suit to gain entry to the established winners. Let's see a deal where both of those aspects come into play.

♠ 8 6
♥ K 7 4
♦ A K Q 7 2
♣ 8 6 3

♠ K Q J 3
♥ 10 9 5
♦ 10 5
♣ Q 10 7 5

♠ 9 7 5 4 2
♥ 8 3
♦ J 8 6 4
♣ J 2

♠ A 10
♥ A Q J 6 2
♦ 9 3
♣ A K 9 4

West leads the ♠K against your small slam in hearts. You win with the ♠A and see that you have three potential losers in your hand – one spade and two clubs. One of these can be discarded on dummy's third diamond winner. You must aim to set up the diamond suit, so that you can discard another of your three initial losers. How can this be done?

Insight: Delay drawing trumps

There are several situations where it is not advisable to draw trumps straight away. This is one of them: you need to use the third round of trumps as an entry to dummy. If you drew all the trumps before setting up the diamonds, you would go down.

Provided diamonds break no worse than 4–2, you can establish the suit with one ruff. The only entry back to dummy, however, will be the king of trumps. So, you cannot afford to draw all the trumps before setting up the diamond suit. After winning the first trick with the ♠A, you should draw two rounds of trumps with the ace and queen. When trumps break 3–2, you leave the last trump out and play the ace and king of diamonds, both defenders following suit. In case diamonds are breaking 4–2, you next ruff a diamond in your hand. You take this ruff with the ♥J, to make sure that West cannot overruff. You then return to dummy with a trump to the king, drawing West's last trump. You can then cash the ♦Q and ♦7, throwing two of your three black-suit losers. Slam made!

Winning the opening lead in the right hand

When you hold the ace and the king in the suit that has been led, it is sometimes important to win the first trick in the right hand. Usually it is right to preserve an entry to the weaker of the two hands. Would you have made 3NT on this deal?

♠ A 5
♥ A K 7 4
♦ A K 8 4
♣ J 5 2

♠ Q 9 8 6 2
♥ 8 6 2
♦ J 10 6 2
♣ 4

♠ J 7 3
♥ Q J 10 9 5
♦ Q 9
♣ A 8 3

♠ K 10 4
♥ 3
♦ 7 5 3
♣ K Q 10 9 7 6

West	North	East	South
–	1♦	Pass	1NT
Pass	3NT	End	

West leads the ♠6 against your contract of 3NT. How will you plan the play?

Suppose you give the matter little thought and play low from dummy, winning East's ♠J with the ♠K. When you play on clubs, East will hold up his ♣A until the third round of the suit. With no entry left to the South hand, you will score only two club tricks. Two tricks in each suit give you a total of eight and, with the diamond suit not breaking 3–3, you will have no way to increase this to nine. One down.

The old maxim, 'plan the contract before playing to Trick 1' is sound advice! Here you start with six top tricks and can easily set up another five tricks in the club suit. In case the defenders can hold up the ♣A for two rounds, you must make sure that you have an entry to your eventual club winners. So, win the opening lead with dummy's ♠A and play on the club suit. East will doubtless hold up the ♣A for two rounds but it will do him no good. Whether or not he then returns a spade, you will be able to reach your hand with the ♠K to score the three established club tricks. Winning the opening lead in the right hand makes the difference between going one down and scoring two overtricks.

Winning with a higher card than is necessary

Sometimes you must win the opening lead with a higher card than is necessary, to preserve a subsequent entry to dummy in the suit. This is a straightforward example:

West	North	East	South
–	–	–	1NT
Pass	3NT	End	

How will you play 3NT when West leads the ♠6?

You play low from dummy and East plays the ♠9. If you win with the ♠J, you will soon regret it. When you turn to the diamond suit,

East will hold up his ace until the third round. Restricted to only two diamond tricks, you will go at least one down.

The contract is easy if you make a plan at the beginning. Five diamond tricks and four top winners outside will bring the total to nine. To ensure that you can reach your winners in the diamond suit, you must win the spade lead with the ace. You clear the diamonds, win East's return and cross to the ♠K to score three more tricks in diamonds. Easy!

Let's see one more example of this important idea:

	♠ 6 4	
	♥ Q 7 3	
	♦ J 7	
	♣ A Q 10 8 5 4	

♠ Q 10 8		♠ J 9 7 2
♥ K J 9 6 2		♥ 8 5
♦ Q 8 4		♦ K 9 6 2
♣ 9 2		♣ K 7 3

	♠ A K 5 3	
	♥ A 10 4	
	♦ A 10 5 3	
	♣ J 6	

West	North	East	South
–	–	–	1NT
Pass	3NT	End	

How will you play 3NT when West leads the ♥6?

The original declarer played low from dummy and won East's ♥8 with the ♥10. When he ran the ♣J, East allowed this card to win. A second round of clubs went to the queen and king. Back came a heart and declarer found that he had no way to reach the four club winners in dummy. He ended two down on a contract that should have been made.

To make the contract, you must preserve the ♥Q as an entry to dummy. You can do this by winning the first trick with the ♥A, rather than the ♥10. East wins the second round of clubs, as before, and can no longer beat the contract. If he returns a heart, dummy's queen will be set up as an entry to the established clubs. If he returns a spade, you will win and lead towards the ♥Q yourself. On a diamond return, you should play low from your hand to ensure a second guard in the suit. When you regain the lead, you will lead towards the ♥Q and the contract will soon be yours. You would make exactly the same play if your hearts were K-10-4. You would win the first trick with the ♥K rather than the ♥10.

POINTS TO REMEMBER

▶ *It is often beneficial to duck an early round (or two) of a suit that you hope to establish. By doing so, you retain the top honour as an entry card.*

▶ *Even when a suit is ready to run if the defenders' cards break evenly, it may be worth ducking the first round. Suppose you have ♦A K Q 7 2 in an otherwise entryless dummy, opposite ♦6 4 in your hand. By ducking the first round, you will score four tricks against a 4–2 break.*

▶ *When you are in a suit contract and hope to establish a side suit in the dummy, it is often necessary to use entries provided by the trump suit. In such a situation you may have to delay drawing trumps. You plan to establish the side suit and then to 'draw trumps, ending in the dummy'.*

▶ *Particularly when you are playing in no-trumps, it can be important to win the opening lead in the right hand. In general, you will want to retain the entry to the hand that began with fewer entries.*

TEST YOURSELF

1

♠ A 3 2
♥ 8 3
♦ J 7 3
♣ A K 9 6 4

♥Q led

♠ K Q J 10 6 5
♥ A K
♦ A 6 2
♣ 5 2

West	North	East	South
–	1♣	Pass	1♠
Pass	2♠	Pass	4NT
Pass	5♥	Pass	6♠
End			

West leads the ♥Q. How will you plan the play?

(The answer is on page 185.)

2

♠ A 6 2
♥ A 10
♦ A 10 8 6 3
♣ 8 5 3

♣Q led

♠ K 5 4
♥ K Q J 9 7 3
♦ 9
♣ A K 2

West	North	East	South
–	1♦	Pass	1♥
Pass	1NT (12–14)	Pass	3♥
Pass	4♥	Pass	4NT
Pass	5♣	Pass	6♥
End			

West leads the ♣Q against 6♥. How will you play the contract?

(The answer is on page 186.)

2

Roman Key-card Blackwood

In this chapter you will learn:
- *how to discover how many aces partner holds*
- *how to discover whether partner holds the king and queen of trumps*
- *how to discover which side-suit kings partner holds.*

The days when 4NT (Blackwood) simply asked how many aces partner held are long since gone. It is recognized nowadays that the king and queen of trumps are equally important cards. So, nearly all tournament players use a 4NT enquiry called Roman Key-card Blackwood (RKCB). The initial responses are based on the five so-called 'key cards', the four aces and the king of trumps.

When a trump suit has been agreed and partner bids 4NT to ask how many key cards you hold, these are the responses:

Roman Key-card Blackwood responses

    5♣   *0 or 3 key cards*
    5♦   *1 or 4 key cards*
    5♥   *2 or 5 key cards without the queen of trumps*
    5♠   *2 or 5 key cards with the queen of trumps*

Suppose you bid 4NT and partner responds 5♣. Nearly always you can tell from partner's previous bidding whether he will hold 0 or

3 key cards. In the occasional situations where you cannot
be sure, you temporarily assume that he has no key cards and
sign off. When he instead holds 3 key cards, he will make
another bid.

···

Insight: The king of trumps

In the original version of Blackwood no special importance
was attached to the king of trumps. You could ask for aces
and then for kings but you would not know which king or
kings partner held. Roman Key-card Blackwood corrects this
omission.

···

Let's see an example of RKCB in action.

West	East	West	East
♠ A K Q 9 3 2	♠ 7 4	1♠	2♥
♥ Q 9 7 2	♥ A K J 8 3	4NT	5♥
♦ A K	♦ 10 7 5	6♥	
♣ 7	♣ Q 10 3		

When West hears a 2♥ response he knows there are only three
possible losers in his hand; the defenders might score tricks
with the ace and king of trumps and the ace of clubs. He bids a
RKCB 4NT to discover how many key cards East holds. The 5♥
response shows two key cards and West therefore bids a
small slam, since one trick is likely to be lost to the key card held
by the defenders.

If East had shown three key cards, via a 5♣ response, West would
have bid a grand slam. If, instead, East had shown only one key
card, with a 5♦ response, West would have stopped at the safe level
of 5♥. Note that West had a perfect hand for using RKCB. The
moment he heard partner's response to 4NT, he would know what
contract to choose.

Let's see an example that illustrates the use of the 5♥ and 5♠
responses, which indicate whether the trump queen is held.

West	East		West	East
♠ A J 9 3	♠ K 4		1♣	1♦
♥ A Q 9 7	♥ K J 8 3		1♥	4NT
♦ 5	♦ A K Q 10 7 2		5♠	6♥
♣ Q J 9 7	♣ 3			

West's 5♠ response shows two key cards (which must be aces here) and the ♥Q. One key card is missing and there is a good chance that this will be the only loser. Note that slam bidding is rarely 100 per cent precise. If West's missing key card was ♠A, there might possibly be two spade losers after a spade lead. However, West might hold the ♠Q or the ♠J, which would lessen the chance of two spade losers. Failing that, the ♠A might be with North or North might fail to lead the suit.

Asking for the queen of trumps

We have already seen that possession of the queen of trumps is shown immediately only when the responder has two (or five) key cards. How can the 4NT bidder check on the trump queen when partner holds a different number of key cards?

> *When the 4NT bidder continues with the cheapest non-trump bid, he asks for the queen of trumps. Without the trump queen, partner signs off in the trump suit. With the trump queen, he cue-bids his lowest side-suit king, otherwise bids 5NT.*

Let's see an example of this:

West	East		West	East
♠ A 9	♠ J 4 2		1♥	3♥
♥ A 10 9 7 3	♥ K Q 8 4		4NT	5♦
♦ A	♦ Q 10 7 2		5♠	6♣
♣ A Q J 9 7	♣ K 4		7♥	

When West hears a double raise in hearts, he can see that the playing strength will be present for a small slam at least. He bids RKCB and hears that partner holds one key card, which must be the ♥K. Already West is happy to play in a small slam. Even if partner holds ♥K-8-5-4 there will be some chance of having no trump loser. If there is a trump loser, the slam may still succeed when East holds the ♣K or the club finesse succeeds.

West is still interested in a grand slam, however. If he bid 5♥ next, this would be a sign-off and partner would pass. West therefore bids 5♠, the cheapest non-trump bid available. This asks East if he holds the queen of trumps. Without the trump queen, East would sign off in 6♥ and West would pass. East actually bids 6♣, which says that not only does he hold the trump queen, he also holds the ♣K. Such a response is music to West's ears! He leaps to 7♥, which will easily be made. If East had bid 5NT, showing the ♥Q but no side-suit king, West would have stopped in 6♥. He would also have stopped at the six-level if East had bid 6♦ to show the ♥Q and the ♦K.

Perhaps you are thinking that this is all a bit complicated. You are right! Still, you can see what an excellent method it is. Instead of guessing whether to bid a slam, you can often be certain whether it is a good idea.

Asking for side-suit kings

Sometimes the response to 4NT tells you that all six important cards (the four aces, the trump king and queen) are held by the partnership. You can then ask for side-suit kings by bidding 5NT. Partner will cue-bid his lowest such king. The following auction arose in the 2005 women's world bridge championship.

West	East	West	East
♠ A K 10 9 2	♠ Q J 8 4 3	1♠	4NT
♥ Q 10 9 7 6 4	♥ A	5♥	5NT
♦ 5	♦ A	6♣	7NT
♣ K	♣ A Q J 10 7 6		

East bid RKCB and found that partner held two key cards, the ace and king of trumps. She continued with 5NT, asking for side-suit kings. With no side-suit kings West would have signed off in 6♠ (returning to the trump suit at the lowest available level). Since West held the ♣K, she responded 6♣ instead. East was now able to count thirteen tricks playing in no-trumps: five spades, two red-suit aces and six clubs. She bid 7NT, which was easily made.

Insight: Identifying the side-suit king

Some players prefer to give a count of their side-suit kings in response to 5NT, as in the original version of Blackwood. This example clearly shows how important it can be to know which king partner holds.

If West had responded 6♥ or 6♦ instead, showing the king of the bid suit, East would have known that there was a potential loser in clubs. She would not have risked bidding a grand slam.

POINTS TO REMEMBER

▶ *In tournament play, most players use Roman Key-card Blackwood instead of normal Blackwood. As with any form of Blackwood, a trump suit has to be agreed. The responses to 4NT then show how many key cards are held:*

    5♣   *0 or 3 key cards*
    5♦   *1 or 4 key cards*
    5♥   *2 or 5 key cards without the queen of trumps*
    5♠   *2 or 5 key cards with the queen of trumps*

▶ *When responder bids 5♣ or 5♦, the 4NT bidder can make the cheapest non-trump bid to ask for the queen of trumps. Responder signs off in the trump suit without the trump queen. Holding the trump queen, he cue-bids his cheapest side-suit king, otherwise bids 5NT.*

▶ *When the 4NT bidder knows that the trump queen is held (along with the other five key cards), he can enquire about side-suit kings by bidding 5NT. Partner will then cue-bid his cheapest side-suit king, otherwise sign off in the trump suit.*

▶ *It's all a bit complicated, yes, but the extra effort is worth it! You can bid many excellent slams and avoid bidding many poor ones.*

TEST YOURSELF

1 *The bidding starts like this:*

West	North	East	South
1♠	Pass	4NT	Pass
?			

Playing RKCB, what will you bid on the following West hands?

a ♠ A Q 10 8 3   **b** ♠ K 10 9 7 2   **c** ♠ J 10 8 6 2
    ♥ 9 2   ♥ A 8 4   ♥ K
    ♦ A J 9 3   ♦ A 8   ♦ A 10 2
    ♣ K 4   ♣ Q J 4   ♣ A K Q 7

2 *The bidding starts like this:*

West	North	East	South
1♥	Pass	2♣	Pass
2♥	Pass	4NT	Pass
5♦	Pass	5♠	Pass
?			

Playing RKCB, what will you bid on the following West hands?

a ♠ 6 3   **b** ♠ K 8 4   **c** ♠ Q 6
    ♥ A Q 9 8 5 2   ♥ A 10 8 7 3 2   ♥ A Q 8 7 5 2
    ♦ Q J 5   ♦ K Q 5   ♦ Q 8
    ♣ K 6   ♣ 4   ♣ Q 10 2

3 *The bidding starts like this:*

West	North	East	South
1♠	Pass	4NT	Pass
5♥	Pass	5NT	Pass
?			

Playing RKCB, what will you bid on the following West hands?

a   ♠ A J 9 7 6 2   b   ♠ A K J 7 3   c   ♠ K J 10 8 7 3
    ♥ A J 8 2   ♥ 4   ♥ K 8 7
    ♦ 5   ♦ Q J 10 4   ♦ A 4
    ♣ K 6   ♣ J 9 3   ♣ K 4

(The answers are on page 187.)

3

Promoting trump tricks in defence

In this chapter you will learn:
- *how to promote a trump trick for partner*
- *how to perform an 'uppercut'*
- *when it is wrong to overruff.*

The most common way of scoring an extra trump trick in defence
is to give partner a ruff. Yes, but you can also promote extra trump
tricks in various situations where declarer or the dummy is also
void in the side suit being led. The most common way of doing
this is to lead a side suit when your partner is in a position to
overruff. If declarer chooses to ruff with a high trump, to prevent
an overruff, this may create an extra trump winner for the defence.
Let's see an example of that.

♠ J 10 6 2
♥ Q 5 4 3
♦ A 10 3
♣ K 5

♠ Q 4
♥ 9 7
♦ Q 8 6 2
♣ Q 8 7 4 2

♠ 5
♥ A K J 2
♦ J 9 7 5
♣ J 10 9 6

♠ A K 9 8 7 3
♥ 10 8 6
♦ K 4
♣ A 3

West	North	East	South
–	–	–	1♠
Pass	3♠	Pass	4♠
End			

Sitting West, you decide to lead the ♥9. This proves to be a lucky choice when East wins with the ♥J. He scores further tricks with the ace and king of hearts and you now need one more trick to beat the contract. Do you see how that trick can be scored?

East continues with the ♥2. What can declarer do? If he ruffs with the ♠9, you will overruff with your ♠Q. If, instead, declarer tries to prevent an overruff by ruffing with the ♠A (or ♠K), your ♠Q will be 'promoted'. What does that mean? It means that its value will be increased so that it subsequently scores a trick. By playing his fourth heart, East achieves what is known as a 'trump promotion'.

Insight: Signalling to partner

Suppose on this deal that West did not hold a promotable trump but instead held the ♣A. A fourth heart might then allow declarer to ruff high and subsequently discard a singleton club on the diamonds. West would discard a high club on the third heart to request a club switch rather than another heart.

Let's see another example of this important technique.

West	North	East	South
–	–	–	1♥
Pass	4♥	End	

Once again you are sitting West. You lead the ♠A and partner encourages a continuation by playing the ♠9. You cash the king and queen of spades successfully, your partner throwing a low diamond on the third round. What now?

You have an excellent chance of a trump promotion if you continue with a fourth round of spades. Look what will happen when the cards lie as in the diagram. If declarer ruffs with dummy's ♥A, to prevent an overruff from East, your ♥Q will become promoted. If, instead, he ruffs with dummy's ♥8, East will overruff with the ♥9. One down either way!

The uppercut

On the two deals we have seen so far, a defender was poised to overruff. You may also be able to promote a trump trick when it is the declarer who will overruff your partner. How can that happen? Your partner ruffs with his highest trump, forcing declarer to overruff with an even higher trump. This may promote the trumps that you hold yourself. Here is a typical example of this spectacular defensive technique.

```
              ♠ 8 7 6 3
              ♥ K Q 7
              ♦ Q 10 6
              ♣ K J 6
  ♠ Q 5           N            ♠ J 4
  ♥ 8 6 4      W     E         ♥ A 10 9 2
  ♦ A K 8 7 5 4    S           ♦ 9 3
  ♣ 7 3                        ♣ 10 8 5 4 2
              ♠ A K 10 9 2
              ♥ J 5 3
              ♦ J 2
              ♣ A Q 9
```

West	North	East	South
–	–	–	1♠
Pass	3♠	Pass	4♠
End			

Sitting West, you lead the ♦A against South's contract of 4♠. Partner encourages with the ♦9 and you continue with the ♦K, everyone following. There are two good reasons to play another diamond now. Firstly, there is a chance of a trump promotion if East can ruff with the ♠J, forcing a higher trump honour from South. Secondly, you want East to ruff dummy's ♦Q anyway, to stop declarer scoring a trick with it.

Insight: The uppercut

An uppercut can succeed even when the lead of the plain suit gives declarer a ruff-and-discard. Suppose you lead the top honours from ♦A-K-Q-7-2, finding partner with a doubleton and declarer with three diamond losers in each hand. The lead of a fourth diamond may allow partner to uppercut.

When you lead a low diamond on the third round, East cannot be absolutely certain that South has no diamonds left (despite the appearance of the ♦J on the second round). Nevertheless, East has nothing to lose by ruffing high – with the ♠J. As it happens, South has to overruff with the ♠K and West's ♠Q is promoted into a trick. East's ♥A will give the defenders a fourth trick and the contract will go one down.

The technique of ruffing high in defence, knocking a big hole in declarer's trump holding, is known as an 'uppercut'.

When it is wrong to overruff

Suppose you are sitting over the declarer, in a position to overruff the lead that partner has just made. Declarer ruffs with the king and your trump holding is A-10-5. Should you overruff? No!

By refusing to overruff, the value of your trump holding will be promoted and you may score a second trump trick. Let's see the situation in the context of a full deal.

```
                    ♠ 8 6 3
                    ♥ Q 7 4 3
                    ♦ Q 10 6
                    ♣ K Q 5
  ♠ A 10 5            N            ♠ 4
  ♥ 8 6          W        E        ♥ A K 10 9 2
  ♦ J 8 5 2          S            ♦ 9 4 3
  ♣ J 7 4 2                        ♣ 10 9 8 3
                    ♠ K Q J 9 7 2
                    ♥ J 5
                    ♦ A K 7
                    ♣ A 6
```

West	North	East	South
–	–	–	1♠
Pass	2♠	Pass	4♠
End			

Sitting West, you lead the ♥8 against South's spade game. Your partner wins with the ♥K and cashes the ♥A. When he continues with the ♥10, declarer ruffs with the ♠K. How should you defend?

If you overruff with the ♠A, the contract will be made! Declarer will win your return and draw your remaining ♠10-5 with his ♠Q-J. Instead, you should refuse to overruff, discarding a diamond or a club. You now hold ♠A-10-5 over South's ♠Q-J-9-7-2. Your trump holding has been promoted and you are certain to score two trump tricks.

Suppose your trumps were slightly weaker: ♠A-9-5. You should still refuse to overruff. This would gain a trick when your partner held the ♠10. Do not overruff when there is any chance that you may promote a second trump trick by discarding instead.

POINTS TO REMEMBER

▶ *When partner is in a position to overruff, you can sometimes create an extra trump trick. Declarer will have to ruff high to prevent an overruff and this may promote the defenders' trump holding.*

▶ *A second way to promote a trump trick is the 'uppercut'. A defender ruffs with his highest trump, forcing declarer to overruff with an even higher trump.*

▶ *Do not overruff a trump honour from a holding such as A-10-5. By discarding instead, you may score a second trump trick with the 10.*

TEST YOURSELF

1

```
                    ♠ A Q J 2
                    ♥ J 10 4 3
                    ♦ Q 7 3
                    ♣ 7 4
   ♦A led        ┌──────────┐      ♠ K 8 6 4
                 │    N     │      ♥ 8 6
                 │  W   E   │      ♦ 10 5
                 │    S     │      ♣ Q 10 8 5 2
                 └──────────┘
```

West	North	East	South
–	–	–	1♥
2♦	3♥	Pass	4♥
End			

Your partner cashes the ♦A, followed by the ♦K. He continues with a third round of diamonds. How should you defend?

2

```
                    ♠ 9 5 3 2
                    ♥ A
                    ♦ K Q 9 4
                    ♣ J 5 3 2
   ♠ K 10 4      ┌──────────┐
   ♥ Q J 8 5 2   │    N     │
   ♦ 6 5 3       │  W   E   │
   ♣ 9 6         │    S     │
                 └──────────┘
```

West	North	East	South
–	–	–	1♠
Pass	3♠	Pass	4♠
End			

You lead the ♣9 against South's contract of 4♠. East wins with the ♣K and cashes the ♣A, the ♣Q falling from South. When East continues with another club, South ruffs with the ♠Q. What is your plan to beat the contract?

(The answers are on page 188.)

4

Keeping the danger hand off lead

In this chapter you will learn:
- *how to finesse into the safe hand*
- *how to duck into the safe hand*
- *how to handle a stopper of A-J-x*
- *when to alter your normal play in a suit*
- *how to make an avoidance play.*

During the play of a hand, particularly in no-trumps, it
often happens that one of the defenders becomes 'safe' while
the other is 'dangerous'. For example, suppose West leads from
a five-card spade suit and you hold up your ♠A until the third
round, exhausting East's spades in the process. West is now the
'danger hand' because if he gains the lead he will cash two spade
tricks. East is the 'safe hand' because he has no spades to play.
You must therefore aim to develop the play without allowing
the danger hand to gain the lead. That is the subject of this
chapter.

Finessing into the safe hand

When you have a choice of finesses to take, you will usually want
to take the finesse that is into the safe hand. Let's see an example of
this technique.

	♠ 5 2		
	♥ A Q 6		
	♦ Q 10 5 3		
	♣ K J 8 3		

♠ K Q J 10 4		♠ 8 7 3
♥ 8 7 5	N	♥ K 10 9 4 2
♦ K 7 2	W E	♦ 9 6 4
♣ 6 2	S	♣ 5 4

	♠ A 9 6	
	♥ J 3	
	♦ A J 8	
	♣ A Q 10 9 7	

West	North	East	South
-	-	-	1NT (15–17)
Pass	3NT	End	

West leads the ♠K against 3NT. You hold up your ♠A until the third round and East follows all the way. How will you continue?

You have eight top tricks: five club tricks and three aces. You can seek a ninth trick by taking a heart finesse or by taking a diamond finesse. Which is the better idea, do you think?

Suppose you cross to dummy with a club and take a diamond finesse, running the ♦Q. You are taking a finesse into the danger hand. If it loses, West will cash two more spade tricks and the contract will go down. Suppose, instead, that you take a heart finesse, running the ♥J. That finesse will lose too, but you will still make the contract! The heart finesse is into the safe East hand. When East wins with the ♥K he will have no spade to play. He will doubtless switch to a diamond, but you can rise with the ♦A and score nine tricks. Dummy's ♥Q will be your ninth trick.

Insight: Avoidance play
The term 'avoidance play' means that you prevent the dangerous defender (the danger hand) from gaining the lead. Finessing into the safe hand is an example of avoidance play.

On that deal you were happy to take a (heart) finesse into the safe hand because even if it lost you would set up an extra trick in the suit. Even when a losing finesse will not set up an extra trick, it can still be right to finesse first into the safe hand. This deal illustrates the situation:

West	North	East	South
–	–	–	1NT (15–17)
Pass	3NT	End	

West leads the ♥4 against 3NT and you win East's ♥10 with the ♥Q. How will you play the contract?

You have eight tricks on top: five diamonds, two aces and the ♥Q. You could set up the extra trick you need with a successful spade finesse or a successful club finesse. Which finesse should you take first?

East is the danger hand because he is the defender who can lead a heart through your remaining ♥K-7. Suppose you run the ♣J, finessing into the danger hand. If the finesse loses you will go down. East will return a heart and West will score four tricks in the suit. Instead, you should cross to the ♦Q and finesse the ♠Q. You are finessing into the safe hand. As it happens, the finesse will win and you will make the contract. Suppose the finesse had lost, though. West could not continue hearts profitably from his side of the table, and after a diamond or spade continuation you would still have the chance to finesse in clubs. By finessing first into the safe hand you would give yourself two chances instead of just one.

Let's look next at a deal where you have a two-way finesse within a single suit.

West	North	East	South
–	–	–	1NT (15–17)
Pass	3NT	End	

West leads the ♠6 against 3NT and you hold up your ace until the third round. How will you play the contract?

You have eight top tricks and must develop another trick from one of the minor suits. This is not a very promising proposition in clubs. Even if the suit divided 3–3, and you could set up a long card by conceding a club trick, there is a big risk that it would be West who gained the lead. He might then be able to cash two spade tricks to beat the contract. No, you should look for your ninth trick in the diamond suit. What is the best play in that suit, do you think?

If West holds the ♦Q, a finesse of dummy's ♦J will succeed. If, instead, East holds the ♦Q, a finesse of your ♦10 will win. Which way should you finesse? You will not fall off your chair when you hear that the best idea is to finesse into the safe hand. Here East is the safe hand because in the dangerous situation where spades break 5–3, East will have no spades left.

So, after winning the third round of spades with the ace, you cash the ♦A and play a low diamond to dummy's jack. As it happens, the finesse loses. No matter. East has no spade to play, so you can win his return and score your nine tricks. (If East did hold another spade, the suit would break 4–4 and you would still make the contract.) Make sure you understand why it was right to finesse into the East hand. By doing so, you would make the contract whether or not the diamond finesse won. If, instead, you were to finesse the ♦10 into the danger hand, you would risk going down if the finesse lost.

Ducking into the safe hand

It often happens that you need to duck a round of a suit in order to establish some tricks in it. When one of the defenders is safe and the other dangerous, you will naturally want to duck into the safe hand. Here is a straightforward example of the play:

West	North	East	South
–	–	–	1NT (15–17)
Pass	3NT	End	

West leads the ♠J against 3NT. How will you play the contract?

You have seven tricks on top and must develop the club suit to provide two more tricks. Suppose you win the spade lead and play ace, king and another club. That's no good! East will win the third round of clubs and may well switch to the ♥Q. You will then lose four heart tricks, going one down.

> ### Insight: Preventing an avoidance play
> When defending, you can sometimes prevent declarer from ducking into the safe hand. Suppose you hold ♦J-10-6 under dummy's ♦K-9-4. When declarer leads a low card towards dummy, you can insert the ♦10 to stop him from playing dummy's ♦9, thereby ducking into the safe hand.

East is the danger hand because he can lead through your ♥K. You must therefore aim to set up the club suit without allowing East on lead. Win the spade lead with the king, cash the ♣K and lead the ♣2 to your ♣10. You are 'ducking into the safe hand'. West wins with the ♣J and cannot attack hearts profitably from his side of the table. You will win his return and score nine tricks: four club tricks and five top winners in the other suits.

How to play a stopper of A-J-x

When you hold A-J-x in the suit that has been led against no-trumps, you can think of your holding as one-and-a-half stoppers. The ace is a certain stopper and the J-x may provide a second stopper. When a low card is led and your right-hand opponent plays the king or the queen, you may need to think carefully whether to take your ace on the first round. The decision will usually depend on which defender is expected to gain the lead. Look at this deal:

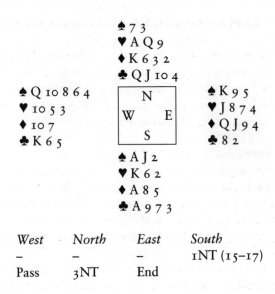

♠ 7 3
♥ A Q 9
♦ K 6 3 2
♣ Q J 10 4

♠ Q 10 8 6 4   ♠ K 9 5
♥ 10 5 3   ♥ J 8 7 4
♦ 10 7   ♦ Q J 9 4
♣ K 6 5   ♣ 8 2

♠ A J 2
♥ K 6 2
♦ A 8 5
♣ A 9 7 3

West	North	East	South
–	–	–	1NT (15–17)
Pass	3NT	End	

West leads the ♠6 against 3NT and East plays the ♠K. How will you play the contract?

Before deciding whether to win with the ♠A, you must make a plan for the whole deal. You have seven top tricks and will therefore need to establish two extra tricks from somewhere. The obvious source of these tricks is in clubs, where you can take a finesse through East. If the finesse wins, there will be no problem; you will have four club tricks, more than enough for the contract. What if the finesse loses? West will then be on lead and you will need to have some protection left in spades. So, you should win with the ♠A immediately. Your remaining ♠J-2 will then act as a stopper in spades (with West on lead). You cross to dummy with the ♥Q and run the ♣Q. This loses to the ♣K but the contract is safe. With West on lead, you still have a guard in the spade suit.

Let's alter the club suit on that last deal, to show that it is not always right to win the first round when you hold an A-J-x stopper:

```
                    ♠ 7 3
                    ♥ A Q 9
                    ♦ K 6 3 2
                    ♣ A 9 7 3
    ♠ Q 10 8 6 4    ┌─────────┐    ♠ K 9 5
    ♥ 10 5 3        │    N    │    ♥ J 8 7 4
    ♦ 10 7        W │         │ E  ♦ Q J 9 4
    ♣ 8 6 5         │    S    │    ♣ K 2
                    └─────────┘
                    ♠ A J 2
                    ♥ K 6 2
                    ♦ A 8 5
                    ♣ Q J 10 4
```

West	North	East	South
–	–	–	1NT (15–17)
Pass	3NT	End	

West again leads the ♠6 to East's ♠K. As before, you will need to develop the club suit to bring your total to nine tricks. The difference here is that it is East who will gain the lead if the club finesse fails. As you see, you will go down if you win the first round of spades. When East wins with the ♣K he will return the ♠9 through your ♠J-2 and the defenders will claim four spade tricks to put you one down.

Insight: Playing a stopper of K-Q-x

You must play a stopper of K-Q-x the same way as with A-J-x. If you expect your left-hand opponent to gain the lead later, you win the first trick and retain the other honour as a second stopper. If instead you expect your right-hand opponent to gain the lead, you will duck the first trick, aiming to remove East's cards in the suit.

You must adopt a different approach – holding up the ♠A until the third round so that you can exhaust East's spades. You allow the ♠K to win. When he returns the ♠9, you insert the ♠J and West wins with the ♠Q. West is welcome to clear the spade suit because when you subsequently take a club finesse East will have no spade to return. (If he did hold another spade, the suit would have broken 4–4 and provide no threat to the contract.)

So, with a stopper of A-J-x you must plan the whole contract, seeing which defender is likely to gain the lead. If it is your left-hand opponent, you will win the first trick. If it is your right-hand opponent, you will hold up the ace until the third round.

Alter your normal play in a suit

Sometimes the normal best play in a suit is to take a finesse. When this would be into the danger hand, it may be prudent to follow a different line, thereby improving your chance of making the contract. Look at the diamond suit on this 3NT contract:

	♠ 7 3	
	♥ A K 9	
	♦ K J 6 3	
	♣ A K 5 3	
♠ 10 6 5	N	♠ K Q J 9 4
♥ J 8 7 3	W E	♥ 10 5 4
♦ 10 9 7	S	♦ Q 8
♣ J 9 6		♣ Q 10 8
	♠ A 8 2	
	♥ Q 6 2	
	♦ A 5 4 2	
	♣ 7 4 2	

West	North	East	South
–	1♣	1♠	1NT
Pass	3NT	End	

West leads the ♠5 against 3NT. How will you play the contract?

You should hold up the ♠A until the third round, to exhaust West's cards in the suit. What then? You have eight top tricks and must develop a ninth trick in one of the minor suits. As we saw on an earlier deal, the odds of doing this in clubs are not good; even if the suit does break 3–3 there is a big risk that East will gain the lead and be able to cash two more spade winners. So, look for your ninth trick in diamonds. What is the best play in that suit?

If you needed four diamond tricks for the contract, you would finesse the ♦J, hoping to find West with ♦Q-x-x (or ♦Q-x). Here you need only three diamond tricks for the contract. You should therefore begin with the king and ace of the suit. If the ♦Q does not fall, little has been lost. You can still lead towards dummy's ♦J on the third round, making the contract when West held the ♦Q all along. All you will have lost is an overtrick. The (huge) benefit comes when East begins with a doubleton ♦Q. The card will fall and you will make the contract where an early finesse would have led to defeat.

Insight: Altering your play in trumps

With a trump holding of ♥A-10-7-2 opposite ♥K-J-9-5-4, you would normally play for the drop. When one defender is a danger hand, you may have reason to alter the normal play, finessing into the safe hand instead. However, the cards lie, you would then keep the danger hand off lead.

Sometimes the normal play in a suit is to play for the drop – when you are missing four cards to the queen, for example. When such a play would risk the danger hand gaining the lead, it may be prudent to take a finesse instead. That's the case on this deal:

♠ 7 3
♥ A 9 6 4
♦ A 4 3 2
♣ K 8 4

♠ A J 9 6 5
♥ Q 8 3
♦ 6
♣ Q 10 7 2

♠ 10 8 4
♥ J 10 7 5
♦ Q 10 8
♣ J 6 5

♠ K Q 2
♥ K 2
♦ K J 9 7 5
♣ A 9 3

West	North	East	South
–	–	–	1NT (15–17)
Pass	2♣	Pass	2♦
Pass	3NT	End	

West leads the ♠6 against 3NT and East plays the ♠10. How will you tackle the contract?

You win the first trick with the ♠Q and see that you have seven top tricks. The diamond suit should provide the two extra tricks that are needed, but it must be developed without allowing East (the danger hand, who can lead through your remaining ♠K-2) to gain the lead.

Suppose you make the 'normal' play in diamonds, cashing the ace and king. You will no longer be able to make the contract! East will gain the lead on the next round of diamonds and a spade return will be fatal. So, you should cross to the ♦A and then finesse the ♦J. As it happens, the finesse will win and you will end with an overtrick. That is not the purpose of the play, however. Even if the finesse had lost to a doubleton ♦Q with West, the contract would be secure. You would still have the four diamond tricks that you need and the safe hand would be on lead, unable to continue spades effectively.

Lead through a defender's high card

Many a contract can be made by the simple technique of leading a low card through a defender's high card towards an honour in the third hand. If the defender plays his high card on thin air he will promote your remaining honours and give you an extra trick. If, instead, he plays low, you can pocket one trick and perhaps turn your attention elsewhere while your protection in the enemy suit remains intact.

It's not easy to visualize, so let's look at a typical deal featuring this technique:

	♠ 7 2	
	♥ K 8 5	
	♦ Q J 5 4	
	♣ A Q 6 4	

♠ 8 5	N	♠ K J 10 9 6
♥ 9 7 3 2	W E	♥ A 10 4
♦ 10 8 7 3	S	♦ A 9 6
♣ 9 7 2		♣ 10 3

	♠ A Q 4 3	
	♥ Q J 6	
	♦ K 2	
	♣ K J 8 5	

West	North	East	South
–	–	1♠	1NT
Pass	3NT	End	

West leads the ♠8 against 3NT. East overtakes with the ♠9 and you win with the ♠Q. How will you play the contract?

You have six top tricks in the black suits and therefore need to score three tricks from the red suits. No red suit on its own is likely to provide three easy tricks. Suppose you lead the ♦K at Trick 2. That's no good. East will win with the ♦A and clear the spade suit. You will score only two red-suit tricks (in diamonds) and East will be able to beat the contract the moment you play on hearts. Your fate will be the same if you play a heart at Trick 2. East will win and clear the spades, again restricting you to eight tricks.

The winning play is to cross to dummy with a club at Trick 2 and to lead a low diamond through East's ♦A towards your ♦K. Do you see the point of this? If East rises with the ♦A on thin air, you will have three diamond tricks, enough for the contract. If, instead, East plays low, as he probably will do, you will score one diamond trick (with the ♦K) without having to release your last spade stopper in exchange. You can then switch to hearts, setting up the second and third red-suit tricks that you need.

Insight: Morton's Fork

The dilemma you inflict on a defender when you lead through his high card is known as Morton's Fork. He is doomed, whether he plays the high card or not. John Morton was Chancellor of England under Henry VII. He said that an outwardly wealthy man should clearly pay high taxes. If a man appeared poor, he must have put his money aside and should therefore pay high taxes too.

The next deal is on the same theme. You lead a low card through the defender's high card. Whether or not he rises with it, you will make the contract.

♠ A K Q J
♥ K J 4 2
♦ 8 5
♣ Q 8 7

♠ 10 8 7 6 3
♥ A
♦ A Q 6 3
♣ A 10 5

N
W E
S

♠ 5 2
♥ 9 8 5
♦ J 10 9 2
♣ J 9 6 4

♠ 9 4
♥ Q 10 7 6 3
♦ K 7 4
♣ K 3 2

West	North	East	South
1♠	1NT	Pass	3♥
Pass	4♥	End	

West leads the ♠6 against your game in hearts. How will you play the contract?

Suppose you win the spade lead, draw trumps and immediately take some discards on the spades. You will go down whichever minor-suit cards you decide to throw. Suppose you throw the ♣3-2. When you play the ♣K to West's ♣A, you will set up the ♣Q as a winner. It will not be much use, though, because you can only throw one diamond from your hand and will still lose two diamond tricks to go down.

To make the contract you must lead a club from the South hand, through West's ace, before deciding what to throw on dummy's spade winners. If West rises with the ace, you will have two club tricks and make the contract easily. If, instead, he plays low, you will discard both your remaining clubs on the spades and not lose a single club trick.

How does the play go? At Trick 2 you lead the king of trumps to West's ace. You win the spade continuation, cross to the queen of trumps and draw East's last trump with the ten. You then lead a low club through West's ace. He will doubtless play low, unwilling to give you two club tricks. You win with dummy's ♣Q and play two more spade winners, throwing your last two clubs. You can then afford to lose two diamond tricks, eventually ruffing the third round of diamonds in dummy to make the game.

So, remember that you can often steal a trick by leading towards an honour, through a high card held by a defender. You may then be able to make the contract whether or not he decides to rise with his high card in the second seat.

POINTS TO REMEMBER

▶ It often happens that one defender is a 'safe hand', the other is a 'danger hand'. When you have a choice of two finesses to take, you should generally prefer the one that is into the safe hand.

▶ Similarly, when you are seeking to establish a suit you should try to duck a trick into the safe hand rather than into the danger hand.

▶ When you have a two-way finesse to take, and can afford to lose a trick in order to set up an extra trick, finesse into the safe hand.

▶ The best play in a suit may be affected by the fact that one of the defenders is a 'danger hand'. For example, you may try to drop the missing honour in the danger hand before eventually playing for the safe hand to hold that card.

▶ You can sometimes steal a trick by leading through a defender's high card towards an honour that you hold.

1

♠ K 5 2
♥ A 6 4
♦ A Q J 4
♣ 8 5 4

♥ J led

♠ A J 10 9 7 3
♥ 2
♦ K 9 7
♣ K 7 3

West	North	East	South
–	1♦	Pass	1♠
Pass	1NT	Pass	4♠
End			

West leads the ♥J against your spade game. How will you play the contract?

(The answer is on page 190. A second problem is overleaf.)

2

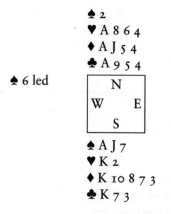

♠ 2
♥ A 8 6 4
♦ A J 5 4
♣ A 9 5 4

♠ 6 led

♠ A J 7
♥ K 2
♦ K 10 8 7 3
♣ K 7 3

West	North	East	South
–	–	–	1♦
Pass	1♥	Pass	1NT
Pass	3NT	End	

How will you play 3NT when West leads the ♠6 and East plays the ♠Q?

(The answer is on page 191.)

5

Weak two-bids

In this chapter you will learn:
- *when to open with a weak two-bid*
- *how to respond to a weak two-bid*
- *the 2NT relay response*
- *how to bid a strong two-bid hand.*

What does an opening bid of 2♦, 2♥ or 2♠ mean? In the early days of bridge such an opening showed a strong hand, in some parts of the world a very strong hand! Indeed, strong two-bids are still in general use when playing rubber bridge. They were described in the companion volume, *Win at Bridge*.

One of the defects of strong two-bids is that they rarely arise. You are not often dealt a hand so powerful that you fear a missed game if you open with a one-bid. In any case, when you hold a really big hand you can open 2♣. So, it is almost universal in tournament bridge to use the opening bids of 2♦, 2♥ and 2♠ to show a weak hand. The hand will be similar in nature to a weak 3♦, 3♥ or 3♠ opening but it will contain a six-card suit rather than a seven-card suit.

> *Open 2♦ when you hold 6–10 points and six diamonds.*
>
> *Open 2♥ when you hold 6–10 points and six hearts.*
>
> *Open 2♠ when you hold 6–10 points and six spades.*

The ideal hand for a weak two-bid will contain a respectable six-card suit. These are all worthy specimens:

a ♠ 6 3   b ♠ K Q J 8 6 2   c ♠ 10 6
   ♥ 10 9 4   ♥ 8 3   ♥ K J 10 8 4 2
   ♦ A Q 10 8 7 4   ♦ K J 2   ♦ 7
   ♣ 7 2   ♣ 10 2   ♣ J 9 5 2

Hand **a** represents a minimum weak 2♦ opening. It is still an ideal weak two-bid because the suit is so strong. Hand **b** is a maximum weak 2♠ bid. Hand **c** contains only five points but the suit is strong and, when non-vulnerable, you would stretch to open with a weak 2♥ bid.

> ## Insight: The strength of a weak two-bid
> Many players nowadays are happy to open at the one-level with ten points and a six-card major suit. For that reason they play that a weak two-bid shows only five–nine points.

Let's look now at three less respectable specimens, ones that contain a defect of some sort. Whether you are willing to open a weak two-bid on such hands depends on your style. If you like to cause the maximum amount of disruption to the opponents' bidding and are willing to accept an increased risk of a bad result of your own, go ahead and open!

a ♠ 6 3   b ♠ J 9 8 6 5 2   c ♠ K Q J 8 3
   ♥ J 9 8 4   ♥ A 3   ♥ 8 7 5
   ♦ K Q 10 9 6 4   ♦ 9 4   ♦ J 7
   ♣ J   ♣ K Q 5   ♣ Q 10 4

Hand **a** contains a four-card major on the side. Many players are unwilling to open a weak-two on such a hand, fearing that they will miss a fit in the major suit. Bear in mind, though, that if you do hold a good heart fit the opponents are likely to hold a big spade fit and may outbid you anyway. Hand **b** is not particularly suitable because only one of the ten points is in the long suit.

You have much more defence to an opponent's contract than partner will imagine. Hand c contains only a five-card suit. Nevertheless, many tournament players would open 2♠. By doing so, they would suggest a good opening lead to partner and make life difficult for the opponents.

You get the idea, then. There is the 'classical weak-two', with everything in order and all the boxes ticked. There is also the 'undisciplined weak-two', which may contain one or more flaws. It is up to you which style you prefer to adopt.

Responding to a weak two-bid

When your partner opens with a weak two-bid, you will have a fairly accurate picture of his hand and can often place the contract immediately. Remember that the opening may be based on quite a weak hand. If you have 12 or 13 points and no particular fit, it will often be right to pass. Against that, when you have a good trump fit, it may be a good move to feign strength and raise partner. You hope to make life even more difficult for the player on your left.

These are the possible responses to an opening 2♥ bid:

2♠ / 3♣ / 3♦	*Natural and forcing*
2NT	*A relay bid to ask for more information*
3♥	*Pre-emptive – partner must pass*
3NT / 4♠	*To play*
4♥	*May be strong; may be pre-emptive*

The responses to 2♦ and 2♠ are along the same lines. We will look at the 2NT relay bid, asking for more information, in a moment. Meanwhile, what response would you make on the hands below?

West	North	East	South
2♥	Pass	?	

a	♠ A K 4	b	♠ K Q 9	c	♠ K 9 7 2
	♥ 6		♥ A 3		♥ 4 2
	♦ Q 10 8		♦ A K J 2		♦ K J 8 2
	♣ A K Q 10 7 2		♣ 10 8 7 2		♣ A J 6

On **a** you can see that 3NT is likely to be a better game than either 4♥ or 5♣. So, respond with a simple 3NT. On **b** you have a 6–2 fit in hearts and can expect there to be good play for a heart game. Respond 4♥. With hand **c** game prospects are poor. Even if partner holds ♥A-K-Q-x-x-x, you are still some way from game. You should therefore pass.

Insight: Trusting partner

When you open with a weak 2♠ or a pre-emptive 3♠, you must trust partner when he responds 3NT. He may well have a running minor suit, which will give him the necessary tricks for 3NT. Remember that partner already knows that you hold six (or seven) cards in your suit for these openings.

The 2NT relay bid

Since a single raise of partner's suit is pre-emptive (2♥ – 3♥, for example), you cannot follow such a route when you wish to make a game try in partner's suit. In such a situation you respond 2NT, a relay bid that asks partner to give you a further definition of his hand. These are the rebids by the opener after a start of 2♦ – 2NT, 2♥ – 2NT or 2♠ – 2NT:

3♣	*Lower-range, suit has 1 (or 0) top honours (A-K-Q)*
3♦	*Lower-range, suit has 2 top honours*
3♥	*Upper-range, suit has 1 (or 0) top honours*
3♠	*Upper-range, suit has 2 top honours*
3NT	*Suit is headed by the A-K-Q*

So, when you are uncertain whether or not to bid game, you respond 2NT. When partner shows an upper-range opening, you can bid game. This is a typical sequence:

West	North	East	South
♠ K Q 9 8 5 3	♠ A 10 4	2♠	2NT
♥ Q 8	♥ K J 6 3	3♠	4♠
♦ Q 10 6	♦ 9 8		
♣ 9 3	♣ A Q J 5		

East holds 15 points and does not expect game to be a good bet opposite a lower-range opening. He responds with the 2NT relay and hears that West is upper-range with two of the three top trump honours. He bids 4♠ and this proves to be a worthwhile prospect.

Bidding is not an exact science. With the East hand we have just seen, game would be a good prospect opposite some lower-range hands; it would be a poor prospect opposite some upper-range hands. Still, you can tilt the odds in your favour by discovering more about the opener's hand.

What if I hold a strong two-bid?

If you normally play strong two-bids, you are no doubt wondering how to cope with such hands when you start to play weak two-bids. The answer is that you must either open with a one-bid, trusting that it will not be passed out, or you must open with a full-blooded 2♣. As a general guideline, lean towards a 2♣ opening when you have a very high point-count. When, instead, you hold a moderate point-count and massive playing strength, it is usually safe to open with a one-bid.

Playing weak two-bids, what opening would you choose on these hands?

a   ♠ A K Q 9 7 2   b   ♠ K 2   c   ♠ A K 9
    ♥ Q J 10 8 7 6   ♥ 3   ♥ A K Q 9 8 6
    ♦ 8   ♦ A K Q J 9 2   ♦ 2
    ♣ –   ♣ A Q J 8   ♣ K Q 6

On hand **a** you want to end in game, yes, but you cannot open 2♣ on a hand with so few high cards and so little defence. Open 1♠ and it will very rarely be passed out. Your intention, given the chance, is to rebid 4♥ to offer partner a choice of games. On **b** you can open 1♦. Someone or other will surely find a bid in one of the majors.

On **c** you will open 2♣. If you open 1♥ you not only risk this being passed out when you have a cold game, you will also find it difficult to bid a slam when partner has modest values and length in one of the black suits.

POINTS TO REMEMBER

▶ A *classical weak two-bid contains 6–10 points and a six-card suit headed by at least one of the three top honours. No four-card major will be held on the side.*

▶ *Some players are happy to open a weak-two when the hand contains one or more flaws. There may be a four-card major on the side, for example; the long major may be weak or contain only five cards; or the high-card strength may be below 6–10 points.*

▶ *A single raise of a weak-two (2♥ – 3♥) is pre-emptive and the opener should not bid again. A game raise (2♥ – 4♥) may be on a strong hand, where you expect to make the contract, or on a weaker hand with four-card trump support. In the latter case, you hope to shut the opponents out from a good contract their way.*

▶ *A response in a new suit is forcing. Responder may also use a relay bid of 2NT. The opener will then reply on a five-step basis, the first two steps showing a lower-range hand with and without two top honours. The next two steps show an upper-range hand with and without two of the three top honours. The fifth step shows A-K-Q in the trump suit.*

TEST YOURSELF

1 *Playing weak two-bids, what opening bid (if any) would you make on the following hands?*

a   ♠ 9   b ♠ A Q 8 2   c ♠ A 8 6
    ♥ 10 2   ♥ K J 10 7 6 4   ♥ J 7 6 5 3 2
    ♦ Q J 10 8 3 2   ♦ 9 3   ♦ 8 2
    ♣ K 9 8 4   ♣ 4   ♣ A 10

2 *What will you respond on the following East hands when your partner opens with a weak two-bid in hearts?*

West	North	East	South
2♥	Pass	?	

a   ♠ 5 3   b ♠ A Q 9 6 4   c ♠ A Q 8
    ♥ A 8 4 2   ♥ 3   ♥ 9 3
    ♦ Q J 10 8 4 2   ♦ A K Q 6   ♦ A 9 7 2
    ♣ 4   ♣ Q 7 3   ♣ Q J 8 2

3 *What will you rebid on the following West hands when your partner has responded with a 2NT relay bid?*

West	North	East	South
2♠	Pass	2NT	Pass
?			

a   ♠ A Q 9 7 6 2   b ♠ K Q 10 8 7 4   c ♠ Q J 10 8 7 2
    ♥ 10 2   ♥ 9 8 6   ♥ J 3
    ♦ J 10 7   ♦ 6   ♦ A J 6 4
    ♣ 9 3   ♣ K J 6   ♣ 5

(The answers are on page 192.)

6

Playing a dummy reversal

In this chapter you will learn:
- *how to play a dummy reversal*
- *how to score the low trumps in the long-trump hand.*

One of the advantages of playing in a suit contract, rather than in no-trumps, is that you can score extra tricks by ruffing. To do this, you normally have to ruff in the short-trump hand. Suppose this is your trump suit:

North
♠ J 7 4

South
♠ A K Q 10 3

You begin with five trump tricks. If you take one ruff in the hand with three trumps, you will score a total of six trump tricks: five in the South hand and one extra for the ruff in dummy. Suppose instead that you ruff something in the long-trump (South) hand. It will not give you an extra trick. It will merely consume one of the trump tricks that you could have scored anyway. So, although there may be some technical reason to ruff in the long-trump hand (for example, you may be trying to set up a side suit in dummy), it will not give you an extra trick directly.

To make sure this is clear, here is a deal that incorporates the trump suit that we have just seen:

```
                    ♠ J 7 4
                    ♥ J 6
                    ♦ A 9 8 3
                    ♣ K 6 5 3
   ♠ 8 6              N              ♠ 9 5 2
   ♥ Q 7 4 2       W     E           ♥ K 10 9 3
   ♦ K Q J 4          S              ♦ 10 6 5 2
   ♣ 10 8 4                          ♣ 9 2
                    ♠ A K Q 10 3
                    ♥ A 8 5
                    ♦ 7
                    ♣ A Q J 7
```

Imagine that you are in 6♠ and West leads the ♦K. How would you play the contract?

You can count 11 top tricks: five rounds of trumps, two red aces and four club tricks. To score a twelfth trick, you must ruff a heart in the short-trump hand (North). So, win the diamond lead and play ace and another heart. You ruff the diamond return, ruff a heart with the ♠J and then draw trumps. You have made six trump tricks and six tricks in the side suits. The slam is yours.

Suppose, instead, you were to ruff one or two diamonds in the long-trump (South) hand. It would not help you at all! You would still make only five trump tricks and leave your total at 11 tricks.

With this important preamble out of the way, we will look at a style of play where you break the normal rule by taking ruffs in the long-trump hand. As we will see, if you can take enough ruffs in the long-trump hand you can actually create an extra trick.

What is a dummy reversal?

If you can take so many ruffs in the long-trump hand that it ends up becoming the short-trump hand, you will score an extra trump trick. Look at this trump suit:

North
♠ Q J 4

South
♠ A K 10 3 2

If you can take as many as three ruffs in the South hand, you will score a total of six trump tricks. You will score three ruffs with the 2, 10 and king, then three trump tricks with the ace, queen and jack. Here is a complete deal where this style of play is necessary.

West	North	East	South
–	1♣	Pass	1♠
Pass	1NT (12–14)	Pass	2♦
Pass	2♠	Pass	4♠
End			

West leads the ♣Q against your game in spades. How will you play the contract?

Suppose first that you look at the losers from the South seat. You have three top losers in hearts and a potential further loser on the fourth round of diamonds. How can you avoid a diamond loser? The main chance is that the diamonds will break 3–3. Another possibility is to draw just two rounds of trumps and continue with the three top diamonds. Playing this way, you would also make the contract when diamonds broke 4–2 but the defender with the doubleton diamond did not hold the last trump. (You would be able to ruff your fourth diamond in the dummy.) Neither of these chances would come home, as the cards lie, and the contract would go down if you played that way.

> ## Insight: The dummy reversal
>
> For a dummy reversal to gain a trick, you must take enough ruffs in your hand to leave dummy with more trumps than you have. If you are playing in a 5–3 trump fit, for example, three ruffs in your hand will leave dummy with three trumps and you with two.

Now look at the losers from the North viewpoint. You still have the three heart losers. If you can ruff the three further potential losers in the club suit, you will make the contract! How should the play go? After winning the club lead, you should ruff a club immediately with the ♠2. You then play the ace and queen of trumps. When trumps break 3–2, you know it is right to continue with the dummy reversal. You ruff another club with the ♠10, return to dummy with the ♦K and ruff dummy's last club with the ♠K. Finally, you return to dummy with the ♦Q, draw the outstanding trump and score the ♦A for your tenth trick. You scored six trump tricks and four side-suit winners.

What if two rounds of trumps had revealed a 4–1 break? It would no longer be possible to play a dummy reversal, since you would not be able to draw trumps after taking three ruffs. You would continue instead with the three top diamonds, hoping that diamonds were 3–3, or the defender with four trumps also held four diamonds.

Scoring the low trumps

Another reason to take ruffs in the long-trump hand is to score the low trumps there. Suppose this is your trump holding:

North
♥ 9 8 2

West
♥ J 10 6 4

East
♥ 5

South
♥ A K Q 7 3

You cannot score five trump tricks simply by drawing trumps, since the defenders' trumps are breaking 4–1. What you need to do is to score the ♥7 and ♥3 by taking ruffs in the long-trump hand. That is the winning line of play on this deal:

♠ K 5 4
♥ 9 8 2
♦ 6 3 2
♣ A K 7 6

♠ J 2
♥ J 10 6 4
♦ K J 5
♣ Q J 10 5

N
W E
S

♠ Q 10 9 8 6
♥ 5
♦ Q 10 8 4
♣ 9 4 2

♠ A 7 3
♥ A K Q 7 3
♦ A 9 7
♣ 8 3

West	North	East	South
–	–	–	1♥
Pass	1NT	Pass	2NT
Pass	3♥	Pass	4♥
End			

West leads the ♣Q and you win with dummy's ♣A. When you play two rounds of trumps, East discards a spade on the second round. You now seem to have three side-suit losers (one in spades, two in diamonds) in addition to a certain trump loser. What can you do about it?

On this particular deal you must look at your winners instead of your losers. You have five winners in the side suits. If you can score all five trumps in your hand, this will bring the total to ten. In other words, you must aim to ruff two clubs in the South hand. How does the play go?

You draw a third round of trumps with the queen, return to dummy with the ♣K and ruff a club with the ♥3. You return to dummy with the ♠K and lead the last club. East shows out and you ruff with the ♥7, West having to follow suit. You score the two aces still in your hand, bringing the total to ten tricks.

You may wonder what happened to the defenders' four 'certain' tricks. The answer is that West will have to ruff his partner's spade winner at the end!

POINTS TO REMEMBER

▶ *Generally speaking, a ruff in the short-trump hand will give you an extra trick. A ruff in the long-trump hand will not produce an extra trick.*

▶ *If you take several ruffs in the long-trump hand (so that it ends with fewer trumps than the hand opposite), you can create an extra trick. Playing in this way is known as 'reversing the dummy'.*

▶ *A dummy reversal may be possible only when the trumps break favourably (because you will eventually have to draw trumps in the short-trump hand). In such a situation you should aim to test the trump suit before embarking on the dummy reversal.*

▶ *It may be beneficial to ruff in the long-trump hand simply with the aim of scoring the low trumps there.*

TEST YOURSELF

1

♠ 8 5 3
♥ A 6 3
♦ A K 7
♣ 10 8 5 4

♦ Q led

♠ A K Q 6 2
♥ K 7
♦ 8 3
♣ A 7 6 3

West	North	East	South
–	–	–	1♠
Pass	2♣	Pass	4♣
Pass	4♠	End	

West leads the ♦Q. You win with the ♦A and draw two rounds of trumps, East throwing a diamond on the second round. How will you continue?

(The answer is on page 193.)

2

♠ K J 9
♥ 8 6 3
♦ A 5 2
♣ A 8 5 2

♣ Q led

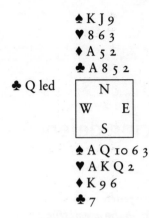

♠ A Q 10 6 3
♥ A K Q 2
♦ K 9 6
♣ 7

West	North	East	South
–	1♣	Pass	1♠
Pass	1NT	Pass	3♥
Pass	3♠	Pass	4NT
Pass	5♣	Pass	6♠
End			

West leads the ♣Q against your small slam in spades. How will you play the contract?

(The answer is on page 194.)

Playing a forcing defence

In this chapter you will learn:
- *how to play a forcing defence*
- *when it is right to hold up the ace of trumps.*

When you are defending, declarer will usually start with more trumps than you do. However, if you can force him to ruff enough times, in the long-trump holding, you may end up with more trumps than he does. This style of play is known as 'playing a forcing defence'. Let's see an example of it.

```
                    ♠ J 10 6
                    ♥ 9 7 6 2
                    ♦ 10 3 2
                    ♣ A Q 5
     ♠ 8 5 4 2          N           ♠ 7
     ♥ A K Q 10 3                    ♥ 8 5
     ♦ A 4         W       E         ♦ 9 8 7 5
     ♣ 10 9           S             ♣ J 8 7 6 4 2
                    ♠ A K Q 9 3
                    ♥ J 4
                    ♦ K Q J 6
                    ♣ K 3
```

West	North	East	South
–	–	–	1♠
2♥	2♠	Pass	4♠
End			

Sitting West, you launch the defence with the ace and king of hearts, everyone following. What now?

Suppose you try your luck with the ♣10. Declarer will win and draw trumps in four rounds. He will then set up the diamonds and claim an easy ten tricks. Instead, you must attack declarer's trump holding, hoping that he started with just five trumps to your four.

Insight: Diagnosing a forcing defence

When you hold four trumps yourself, it is easy to see that a forcing defence may succeed. Look also for situations where you hold only one trump and suspect from the bidding that your partner will hold four trumps. In this case too a forcing defence may be promising.

After cashing two top hearts, you should continue with another heart winner. Declarer ruffs and now has the same number of trumps as you. He can no longer make the contract! He will doubtless draw two rounds of trumps, discovering the 4–1 trump break. If he draws your remaining two trumps, he will have no trumps left in his own hand. When you win with the ♦A you will be able to cash two heart winners.

What will happen if declarer chooses instead to play on diamonds without drawing your trumps? You will win and play yet another heart, forcing him to ruff again. You will then have two trumps to declarer's one. He will have 'lost trump control' and will go down.

Always consider a forcing defence when you hold four trumps (or suspect that partner does). By leading your own strongest side suit, you may be able to force declarer to ruff.

Holding up the ace of trumps

A trump holding of four cards to the ace is particularly valuable when you are considering a forcing defence. One reason is that

you will be able to force declarer again when you win with the ace
of trumps. Sometimes, though, you must calculate carefully when
you should take the trump ace. This type of hand is quite common:

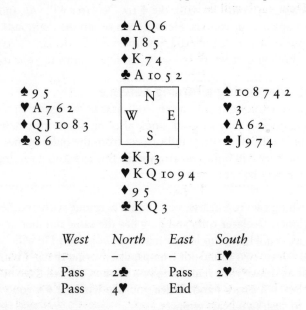

♠ A Q 6
♥ J 8 5
♦ K 7 4
♣ A 10 5 2

♠ 9 5
♥ A 7 6 2
♦ Q J 10 8 3
♣ 8 6

♠ 10 8 7 4 2
♥ 3
♦ A 6 2
♣ J 9 7 4

♠ K J 3
♥ K Q 10 9 4
♦ 9 5
♣ K Q 3

West	North	East	South
–	–	–	1♥
Pass	2♣	Pass	2♥
Pass	4♥	End	

Sitting West, you embark on a forcing defence by leading the ♦Q.
Since declarer knows that you would not lead the queen from a
holding headed by the A-Q-J, he places the ♦A with East. He plays
low from dummy on the first round of diamonds and low again
on the second round. (This would be the winning play if East held
a doubleton ♦A.) You continue with a third round of diamonds,
covered by the ♦K and ♦A, and declarer ruffs. How will you
continue the defence when declarer leads the ♥K at Trick 4?

Suppose you win with the ♥A. The contract will then be made.
A fourth round of diamonds will not continue the 'forcing defence'
because declarer will be able to ruff in dummy (in the short-trump
holding). He will then be able to draw trumps and make the
remaining tricks. So, how can you do better in defence?

When you take your ♥A you want to be able to continue your
attack on the trump length in declarer's hand. You can do this

66

only if you hold up your ace of trumps until the third round, when dummy's trumps will be exhausted. So, allow declarer's king to win the first round of trumps. When he plays another trump, duck again. These cards will be left:

♠ A Q 6
♥ 8
♦ –
♣ A 10 5 2

♠ 9 5
♥ A 7
♦ 8 3
♣ 8 6

N
W   E
S

♠ 10 8 7 4
♥ –
♦ –
♣ J 9 7 4

♠ K J 3
♥ Q 10
♦ –
♣ K Q 3

Declarer has an unhappy look on his face. If he plays the ♥Q, you will win with the ♥A and play another diamond, forcing declarer to ruff (in what was the long-trump hand) with the ♥10. Your ♥7 will be the last trump out and you will also score a diamond to put the game two down. The best that declarer can do is to abandon trumps and to play black-suit winners instead. You will score a ruff with the ♥7 and that will be one down.

Insight: Holding up the ace of trumps

There are other situations where it may work well to hold up the ace of trumps. Declarer will often wish to draw precisely two rounds of trumps at the start of play. If you hold up the ace from A-x-x on the first round, you can draw a second and third round of trumps if declarer continues the suit.

So, when you are playing a forcing defence and hold four trumps to the ace, think carefully when to take the ace of trumps. Do not take it early if the dummy will then have a trump left that can be used to ruff the side suit that you are using for the forcing defence.

POINTS TO REMEMBER

▶ *When you hold four trumps, consider playing a forcing defence. This means you lead your strongest side suit, hoping to force declarer to ruff. If declarer can be made to ruff twice, you may end up with longer trumps than he has.*

▶ *When you hold four trumps to the ace, do not take the ace of trumps on the first or second round if this will mean that declarer can use the short-trump holding (in dummy) to avoid being forced in the long-trump holding.*

▶ *Sometimes the opponents' bidding suggests that they are in a 4–4 fit. If you hold only one trump yourself, your partner will hold four trumps and a forcing defence may be successful.*

TEST YOURSELF

1

♠ A 10 7
♥ 7 6 4 3
♦ K J 5
♣ K 9 7

♠ 8 5 3 2
♥ K J 8 2
♦ A 8 4
♣ 6 4

West	North	East	South
–	–	–	1♠
Pass	3♠	Pass	4♠
End			

Sitting West, you embark on a forcing defence by leading the ♥2.
East wins with the ♥A and continues with the ♥10 covered by
South's ♥Q and your ♥K. When you play the ♥J, declarer ruffs and
plays the ace and king of trumps, partner discarding a diamond on
the second round. Declarer then leads the ♦2 from his hand. How
will you defend?

(The answer is on page 195. A second problem is overleaf.)

2

♠ 7 4 3
♥ 9 7 5
♦ A J 3
♣ Q 9 7 5

♠ A K 8 6
♥ K Q J 8 2
♦ 10 9
♣ 6 4

West	North	East	South
–	–	–	1♠
2♥	2♠	3♥	4♠
End			

You lead the ♥K, winning the first trick, and South ruffs the heart continuation. When he leads the ♠Q you win with the ♠K and East discards a low club. What is your plan for the defence?

(The answer is on page 196.)

8

Negative, responsive and competitive doubles

In this chapter you will learn:
- *how to use a negative double*
- *how to use a responsive double*
- *how to use a competitive double*.

In the early days of bridge, the call of 'double!' had only one meaning. It indicated that you thought the opponents' contract would go down and that you wanted to increase the stakes. It was soon realized, particularly at low levels of the auction, that there was a more useful meaning for a double. It should ask partner to choose a trump suit. This is the familiar take-out double. In all the following auctions the double is for take-out, asking partner to choose between the unbid suits:

	West	*North*	*East*	*South*
a	1♥	Pass	Pass	Dble
b	1♦	Pass	1♠	Dble
c	3♣	Dble		
d	1♥	Pass	2♥	Dble

You may wonder which doubles are still for penalties. A double of a weak 1NT opening is a penalty double. (A penalty double of a strong 1NT is less valuable and some players use the call with a conventional meaning.) Most doubles of a game contract are for penalties. In rubber bridge a double in the following type of auction is also for penalties:

	West	North	East	South
e	1♥	2♣	Dble	

Even this double, though, is no longer played for penalties by the majority of tournament players. They play a double of an overcall for take-out, usually showing the two unbid suits. Such a double is known as a 'negative double'. Let's take a look at it.

The negative double

Look at this bidding problem:

West	West	North	East	South
♠ 9 3 2	–	–	1♣	1♠
♥ A J 8 2	?			
♦ Q 9 6 2				
♣ Q 7				

Your partner opens 1♣ and South overcalls 1♠. What do you bid?

If a double would be for penalties, as at rubber bridge, there would be no good answer to the question. You cannot bid 1NT because you have no stopper in spades. Nor are you strong enough to bid 2♦, which would be forcing and carry your side too high when partner was minimum.

Tournament players have solved this problem by using a double of an overcall for take-out. A double here would strongly suggest four cards in the other major (hearts) and show enough points to contest the auction at this level. The opener would choose a rebid to describe the nature of his hand. With a heart fit, for example, he would rebid 2♥ with a hand in the minimum range, 3♥ or 4♥ with a stronger hand.

You can see how useful such a meaning for the double can be. Do you lose very much by not being able to double for penalties? Not at this level, certainly! When was the last time that you held such good spades that you thought the best contract for your side was one spade doubled? It would not happen very often. In any case, there is still a way to catch the opponents, as we will see in a moment.

It is best to play that doubles of an overcall are negative (for take-out) up to the level of 3♠. Let's see a hand where you might want to use a negative double at that level:

West	West	North	East	South
♠ 9 3	–	–	1♦	3♠
♥ A J 8 2	?			
♦ Q 9 6				
♣ A Q 7 3				

Without a negative double at your disposal you would, again, be completely stuck. Here you enter the auction with a negative double and wait to hear what partner says next. He may hold four hearts with you and be able to rebid 4♥. Perhaps he has a spade stopper and can rebid 3NT. If he has neither of these, and no special distribution, he may even choose to pass your double, deciding that it will be best to take a penalty against the 3♠ contract.

What happens when your partner opens the bidding and the next player overcalls in a suit that you hold strongly? You would like to make a penalty double but ... oh dear ... you have agreed to play negative doubles with your partner. All is not lost! Suppose you hold the North cards on this typical deal:

```
                    ♠ 9 3
                    ♥ Q 7 5
                    ♦ A J 9 3
                    ♣ K 10 8 6
    ♠ J 4                           ♠ K 10 8 6
    ♥ 10 6              N           ♥ K 8 3 2
    ♦ K Q 10 8 5 4   W   E         ♦ 7 6
    ♣ A J 7              S          ♣ 4 3 2
                    ♠ A Q 7 5 2
                    ♥ A J 9 4
                    ♦ 2
                    ♣ Q 9 5
```

West	North	East	South
–	–	–	1♠
2♦	Pass	Pass	?

West overcalls 2♦ and, sitting North, you would like to make a penalty double. Since you are playing negative doubles, this is not possible. In such a situation, when you have a stack of trumps sitting over the overcaller, you should pass instead. If the next player passes, your partner will be able to picture the situation. He is short in diamonds himself and East did not raise the overcall. The odds are high indeed that you are sitting with a good diamond holding but could not make a penalty double. South should therefore double himself. Such a double is for take-out but is made in the hope (expectation) that partner will pass for penalties.

As you see, then, you are not paying a high price to use negative doubles. On a large proportion of the hands where you would have liked to be playing a double for penalties, your partner will re-open the bidding with a take-out double, which you will be able to pass.

The responsive double

Let's look next at yet another type of double, one that is in common usage even in rubber bridge. It is known as a 'responsive double' and arises when your partner has made a take-out double and responder raises the opener's suit before you have had a chance to reply to partner's double. This is a typical situation:

West	West	North	East	South
♠ 10 3 2	–	1♥	Dble	2♥
♥ 8 4	?			
♦ K Q 9 6				
♣ A J 7 2				

What should you bid now? With ten points you are worth a response. Suppose you respond 3♣, though. You may find that partner holds only three clubs and you had a 4–4 diamond fit. It's the same if you guess to respond 3♦. You may find that you had a better fit in clubs.

The answer is for you to make a further double yourself. Since this is in response to partner's take-out double, the call is known as a 'responsive double'. It is for take-out and asks partner to choose a trump suit. On this particular auction, partner's original double strongly suggests that he holds four spades (because spades is the 'other major'). If you held four spades yourself, you could be fairly sure that you and your partner held a 4–4 fit there. You would therefore respond 2♠ (or perhaps 3♠ or 4♠, with a stronger hand). It follows that when you make a responsive double instead you are likely to hold the two minor suits.

Again it makes good sense to play responsive doubles up to and including the level of 3♠. Following is a hand when you might make such a high-level responsive double.

West	West	North	East	South
♠ J 3	–	1♠	Dble	3♠
♥ 7 4	?			
♦ A Q 10 6 2				
♣ A 10 8 4				

Once again your best move is to double – a responsive double. With four cards in hearts you would bid 4♥ instead, expecting there to be a 4–4 fit in the suit. Your double therefore suggests length in the minor suits. You hope that partner has a spade stopper and will be able to bid 3NT. The higher the bidding is, of course, the greater the strength you will need in order to compete with a negative double. After a start of 1♣ – Dble – 2♣, you might make a responsive double on as little as seven points. You are only forcing the bidding to the two-level, after all.

Do you lose much by treating such a double as for take-out? Not really. It is hardly attractive to double the opponents for penalties when they have found a good fit. You will usually do at least as well by choosing trumps yourself.

The competitive double

We will end the chapter by looking at another situation where the opponents have found a fit and a penalty double will rarely be worthwhile. Look at this bidding problem:

West	West	North	East	South
♠ 9 3	–	1♠	2♦	2♠
♥ A Q 8 3	?			
♦ J 2				
♣ K J 8 7 4				

You are reluctant to pass, with 11 points facing a two-level overcall. What can you bid, though? It is hardly satisfactory to bid 3♣ on such a moderate suit. The answer is to make a take-out double. In this situation, when partner has overcalled and the third player has raised, the call is known as a 'competitive double'. It suggests tolerance for partner's suit (usually a doubleton) and length in the two unbid suits.

All options are open to your partner at his next turn. He can show a fit for one of your suits, he can rebid his own suit if that seems best, or he can pass the double for penalties. This last option is very much an exception and not at all the purpose of your double. Partner will rarely pass a competitive double at the two level. After a start of 1♠ – 2♦ – 3♠ – Dble, however, he would be more likely to conclude that the best option was to defend.

POINTS TO REMEMBER

▶ *In tournament play it is common to use the 'negative double'. A double of an overcall, up to the level of 3♠, is for take-out. It strongly suggests that you hold any unbid major suit(s).*

▶ *When you are playing negative doubles, the opener will usually re-open with a take-out double when left-hand opponent's overcall runs back to him. This is to cater for the situation where partner has a strong holding in the overcaller's suit but was unable to make a penalty double.*

▶ *In all types of bridge, players use the 'responsive double'. When your partner doubles a one-bid for take-out and the next player raises this to the two- or three-level, a double by the fourth player is a responsive double, for take-out.*

▶ *In tournament play, it is common to use the 'competitive double'. When your partner has overcalled, and the third player raises his partner to the two- or three-level, a double by the fourth player is 'competitive'. It suggests tolerance for partner's suit and length in the unbid suits.*

TEST YOURSELF

1 *Playing negative doubles, you are East and the bidding starts:*

West	North	East	South
1♥	2♦	?	

What will you bid on the following East hands?

a ♠ Q 10 8 3
   ♥ 9 2
   ♦ 7 5 3
   ♣ A K J 4

b ♠ J 9 3 2
   ♥ A 8 4
   ♦ 10 8 6
   ♣ Q 10 4

c ♠ A 7 6
   ♥ 6 5
   ♦ A Q 10 7 2
   ♣ J 8 3

2 *Playing responsive doubles, you are sitting South and the bidding starts like this:*

West	North	East	South
1♥	Dble	2♥	?

What will you bid on the following South hands?

a ♠ 10 3
   ♥ 9 8 2
   ♦ A J 5 3
   ♣ K Q 6 4

b ♠ A J 9 3
   ♥ 8 4
   ♦ K Q 6
   ♣ J 9 7 3

c ♠ 7 6
   ♥ A Q J 8
   ♦ 10 9 7 2
   ♣ Q 8 2

3 *Playing competitive doubles, you are sitting South and the bidding starts like this:*

West	North	East	South
1♥	2♣	2♥	?

What will you bid on the following South hands?

a ♠ A J 10 3
   ♥ 8 3
   ♦ K 10 9 7 4
   ♣ Q 4

b ♠ K 7 6 2
   ♥ 9 4
   ♦ 10 6 5 3
   ♣ K 10 4

c ♠ K 9 4 2
   ♥ A J 10 8
   ♦ J 9 7 2
   ♣ 6

(The answers are on page 197.)

9

Elimination play

In this chapter you will learn:
- *how to perform an elimination play*
- *how to perform a loser-on-loser elimination.*

Has it ever occurred to you that it is never an advantage to make the first play in a suit? You will always do at least as well, often better, if you can persuade the defenders to make the first play. Let's see a couple of single-suit positions that illustrate this.

North
♦ Q 5 3

West   *East*
♦ K 10 8 2   ♦ A 9 7

South
♦ J 6 4

Suppose you need one diamond trick and have to attack the suit yourself. You would lead towards one honour and then towards the other. Your main chance of success would be to find one defender holding both the ace and king. When the cards lie as in the diagram, you would fail to score a diamond trick. If, instead, the defenders had to make the first play, you would be assured of a trick from the suit. The defender in third seat would have to rise with the ace or king and your queen-jack would then be worth a trick.

Sometimes forcing the defenders to open a suit will save you a guess. Look at this club position:

                          North
                          ♣ K J 6
          West   *East*
          ♣ Q 8 4   ♣ 9 7 5 3
                          South
                          ♣ A 10 2

When you have to make the first play yourself, you can score three tricks from the suit only if you can guess which defender holds the ♣Q. When the defenders make the first play in the suit, you are certain to score three tricks.

Performing an elimination play

So, let's agree that with some holdings you would very much like the defenders to make the first play in the suit. How can you force them to do this? You do so by throwing a defender on lead after you have removed all his other possible plays. You 'eliminate' or remove from play the trumps and the other side suits, forcing the defender to play the only remaining suit (or give you a ruff-and-discard). It's not easy to imagine, perhaps, so let's look at a full deal.

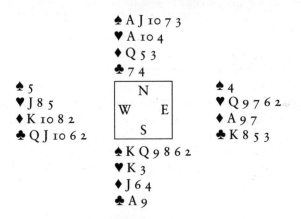

```
                    ♠ A J 10 7 3
                    ♥ A 10 4
                    ♦ Q 5 3
                    ♣ 7 4
    ♠ 5                   N                ♠ 4
    ♥ J 8 5                                ♥ Q 9 7 6 2
    ♦ K 10 8 2       W         E           ♦ A 9 7
    ♣ Q J 10 6 2          S                ♣ K 8 5 3
                    ♠ K Q 9 8 6 2
                    ♥ K 3
                    ♦ J 6 4
                    ♣ A 9
```

West	North	East	South
–	–	–	1♠
Pass	4♠	End	

West leads the ♣Q against your spade game. How will you play the contract?

This is the diamond suit that we saw on the previous page. As declarer, you would like to force the defenders to play diamonds for you. This can easily be done! You win the club lead and draw trumps in three rounds.

The next move is to play the king and ace of hearts and then to ruff a heart. What is the purpose of this? By removing the hearts from your own hand and the dummy (eliminating the hearts, in other words), you prevent the defenders from safely playing this suit later. If they did play a fourth round of hearts, this would give you a ruff-and-discard; you could ruff in one hand and discard a diamond loser from the other.

Insight: Safe ruff-and-discard

Suppose declarer has a side suit of ♦A-J-6-2 opposite ♦K-10-5-3 and hopes to save himself a queen guess with an elimination play. If a defender leads a diamond when he is thrown in, this will indeed help declarer. But a lead of some other suit, giving a ruff-and-discard, will not help him at all! Look out for this situation when defending.

After drawing trumps and eliminating the heart suit, you will have reached this position:

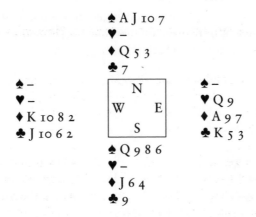

♠ A J 10 7
♥ —
♦ Q 5 3
♣ 7

♠ —
♥ —
♦ K 10 8 2
♣ J 10 6 2

N
W E
S

♠ —
♥ Q 9
♦ A 9 7
♣ K 5 3

♠ Q 9 8 6
♥ —
♦ J 6 4
♣ 9

Now you exit (in other words, give up the lead) by playing a club. It makes no difference which defender wins this trick. He will then have only two possible plays to make. One losing option will be to make the first lead in the diamond suit, restricting your losers there to just two. The other losing option will be to give you a ruff-and-discard. You will ruff in one hand or the other and throw a diamond loser from the opposite hand. Again you will lose just two diamond tricks and make the contract.

Suppose you showed your local expert the full diagram on the previous page and asked him how he would play Four Spades on a club lead. He would reply: 'No problem there! I will draw trumps, eliminate the hearts and exit in clubs. The defenders will then have to open the diamonds or give a ruff-and-discard.'

Don't worry if elimination play is new to you and seems a bit difficult. Once you have performed a few elimination plays – and opportunities for doing so are frequent – it will soon become automatic.

Exiting in the key suit itself

On the deal we have just seen, you exited in one suit (clubs) and forced a defender to play on another (diamonds). Sometimes you exit in the key suit itself. That's what happens here:

♠ A Q 10 7 3
♥ 6 5 3
♦ 7 6
♣ A K 2

♠ 8 4
♥ K J 9 2
♦ J 10 9 2
♣ Q 8 5

♠ 5
♥ 8 7 4
♦ Q 8 5 3
♣ J 10 9 7 3

♠ K J 9 6 2
♥ A Q 10
♦ A K 4
♣ 6 4

You bid to Six Spades and West leads the ♦J. How will you play the contract?

Your general plan will be to eliminate both the minor suits and then to play a heart to the ten. If West wins with the ♥J, he will have to return a heart into your ♥A-Q tenace or give you a ruff-and-discard. So, what are the steps involved in this?

You win the first trick with the ♦A and draw trumps in two rounds. You cash the ♣A-K and ruff a club in the South hand, eliminating the club suit. You then play the ♦K and ruff a diamond in dummy, eliminating the diamond suit. The lead is in dummy and these cards remain:

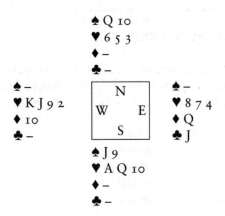

♠ Q 10
♥ 6 5 3
♦ −
♣ −

♠ −   N   ♠ −
♥ K J 9 2   W   E   ♥ 8 7 4
♦ 10   ♦ Q
♣ −   S   ♣ J

♠ J 9
♥ A Q 10
♦ −
♣ −

Now you play a heart to the ten. The finesse loses to the ♥J but
West is end-played. He will have to play a heart into your ace-
queen tenace or give you a ruff-and-discard.

Insight: Preventing a throw-in

Suppose on this deal that declarer held ♥A-Q-8 instead of
♥A-Q-10. If he is allowed to play a low heart to the 8, he will
succeed as before. To prevent such a throw-in, the defender
in second seat must rise with the 9 (or higher card) to force
declarer to play the queen.

The loser-on-loser elimination play

So far we have seen two different ways of throwing a defender on
lead. The first arose when, in one side suit, you had a low singleton
left in each hand. You exited in that suit, eliminating it at the same
time. The second method was to lose the first round of the suit in
which you were hoping to gain a trick. We will now look at a third
method, a somewhat exotic one. You lead a loser from one hand
and, instead of ruffing it, you discard a loser from some other suit.
Look at the following deal.

♠ Q J 10 6 3
♥ A Q 7 3
♦ 6 5 3
♣ 8

♠ 5
♥ J 9 6 2
♦ K 10 7 2
♣ Q J 10 6

♠ 9 4
♥ 10 5
♦ J 9 8
♣ K 9 5 4 3 2

♠ A K 8 7 2
♥ K 8 4
♦ A Q 4
♣ A 7

You reach Six Spades and West leads the ♣Q. How will you plan the play?

You have two potential losers in diamonds. If the heart suit breaks 3–3, dummy's thirteenth heart will become good and you will be able to discard the ♦4. If hearts do not break 3–3, you could fall back on a finesse of the ♦Q. Is there anything better?

Indeed there is! When West holds four or more hearts, you can guarantee the contract. You win the club lead with the ace and draw trumps in two rounds. You then ruff the ♣7 in dummy, eliminating that suit. Next you play the king, ace and queen of hearts. The suit does not break 3–3, but you are pleased to see that it is West who holds four hearts. This means that you can end-play him. These cards are left:

♠ J 10
♥ 7
♦ 6 5 3
♣ –

♠ –
♥ J
♦ K 10 7 2
♣ J

♠ –
♥ –
♦ J 9 8
♣ K 10 9

♠ K 8 7
♥ –
♦ A Q 4
♣ –

You lead the ♥7 (a loser) and discard the ♦4 (another loser). You are making what is known as a 'loser-on-loser play'. The effect of it here will be splendid. West will be left on play and will have to lead a diamond from his king into your ace-queen tenace, or give a ruff-and-discard. In both cases you will have 12 tricks and your slam.

Suppose East had started with four hearts. It would not then help you to lead the fourth heart, discarding a diamond loser. East would be left on play and could lead a diamond through the ace-queen.

POINTS TO REMEMBER

▶ To perform an elimination play, you draw trumps and eliminate one or two of the side suits. You then throw a defender on lead, forcing him to make the first play in the remaining side suit or give a ruff-and-discard.

▶ Sometimes you throw a defender on lead on the first round of the suit in which you are hoping to gain a trick. For example, you might lead to the jack in an A-J-10 combination.

▶ Another possibility is to lead a loser in one suit and to discard a loser from a different suit. You gain because the defender thrown on lead will have to give you a trick with his return.

TEST YOURSELF

1

♠ K Q 7
♥ A 10 8 6 3
♦ J 5 3
♣ 6 4

♣10 led

N
W   E
S

♠ A 8 4
♥ K 9 7 5 2
♦ Q 6 2
♣ A K

West	North	East	South
–	–	–	1♥
Pass	4♥	End	

West leads the ♣10 against your heart game. You win and play the ♥K, East showing out on the first round. How will you continue?

(The answer is on page 198. A second problem is overleaf.)

2

             ♠ Q 10 8 3 2
             ♥ A 9 2
             ♦ 7 5 3
             ♣ K 4

♥Q led

	N	
W		E
	S	

             ♠ A K J 9 7 5
             ♥ 8
             ♦ A J 10
             ♣ A 10 3

West	North	East	South
–	–	–	1♠
Pass	4♠	Pass	6♠
End			

West leads the ♥Q against your spade slam. How will you play the contract?

(The answer is on page 199.)

10

....

Bidding the opponent's suit

In this chapter you will learn:
- *how to show a strong raise after an enemy overcall*
- *how to show a strong raise of partner's overcall*
- *how to show a strong hand opposite a take-out double.*

As you know, bids can be made in only five denominations:
no-trumps and the four suits. Suppose an opponent has bid hearts.
If you and your partner never make any subsequent bids in hearts
yourselves, you will be greatly restricting your bidding vocabulary.

Tournament players are unwilling to restrict themselves in this
way. They like to make full use of every available bid! What do
you think a bid in the opponent's suit should mean? In general, it
shows a strong hand of some sort and in this chapter we will see
the most important uses of such bids.

_____

Showing a strong raise after an overcall

Suppose your partner opens 1♥ and the next player overcalls 1♠.
When you hold four-card heart support you would like to raise
the bidding as high as you dare, to restrict the bidding space
available to the opponents. When you make such a pre-emptive
raise, you don't want partner to think that you have a good hand
and perhaps carry the bidding to an expensive level. So, you would
like to be able to tell partner, 'I have a weak hand but I am bidding

high to make life difficult for the other side'. It can be done! This is the scheme of responses when your partner's opening bid has been overcalled:

West	North	East	South
1♥	1♠	?	

East responds along these lines:

2♥	*three-card raise and about 5–9 points*
3♥	*four-card raise and about 4–8 points, pre-emptive*
4♥	*five-card raise and about 5–9 points, pre-emptive*
2♠	*sound high-card raise to at least 3♥.*

As you see, on any hand that is worth a genuine game try, based on high-card values, you begin with a cue-bid in the opponent's suit.

Using this method, which is almost universal in tournament play, what would you respond (after the auction shown above) on the following East hands?

	a	b	c
♠	10 3	9 8	A 10 6
♥	K 8 2	A J 8 4	Q J 8 2
♦	10 8 7 5	10 8 6 3 2	J 2
♣	K J 6 4	7 6	K 9 5 2

You raise to 2♥ on **a** and make a pre-emptive raise to 3♥ on **b**. Hand **c** represents a genuine high-card raise to 3♥, so you begin with a cue-bid of 2♠.

Perhaps you are not particularly impressed by this. You should be! It is one of the most important developments in bidding in the last two decades or so. When you have a good fit for partner but little overall strength, it is important to deny your opponents bidding space with a pre-emptive raise. By raising to 3♥ on hand **b**, for example, you rob the fourth player of the chance to raise his partner to 2♠. If he then has to bid 3♠ on hands that are really worth only a single raise to 2♠, as well as those worth a sound raise to 3♠, his partner will have no accurate picture of what strength lies opposite.

Let's look at the situation from the opener's point of view. Suppose your opening bid is overcalled and partner shows a sound raise, by making a cue-bid. You should sign off at the minimum level, when you would have rejected a normal double-raise game try (1♥ – 3♥, for example) had there been no intervention. This is a typical auction:

West	East	West	North	East	South
♠ K J 4 3	♠ Q 10 2	1♥	2♣	3♣	Pass
♥ A Q 8 5 2	♥ K J 6 3	3♥	End		
♦ Q 6	♦ A 7 4				
♣ 9 3	♣ J 10 5				

East shows a sound high-card raise to the three-level and West signs off. West's ♦Q-6 is worth very little. Had he held ♦K-6 instead, he would probably have rebid 4♥ instead of 3♥. Now look at the East hand. Had his clubs been ♣K-10-5, he would still have begun with a cue-bid (because a raise to 4♥ would suggest a moderate hand with five-card support). However, with 13 points he would then have raised partner's 3♥ sign-off to 4♥.

Showing a strong raise of partner's overcall

Exactly the same principle applies when your partner has made an overcall. With three-card support (particularly when you hold an honour in partner's suit) you will usually give a single raise to remove bidding space from the opponents. You should raise even when your hand is quite weak. With four-card support, you should aim to raise a one-level overcall to the three-level, again even when quite weak.

This is the general scheme, when partner has overcalled:

West	North	East	South
1♦	1♠	Pass	?

Sitting South, you respond along these lines:

2♠	*three-card raise and about 5–9 points*
3♠	*four-card raise and about 4–8 points*
4♠	*five-card raise and about 5–9 points*
2♦	*sound high-card raise to at least 2♠.*

You expect partner to hold five spades for his overcall. In general, you add the number of cards you hold in support and raise to the appropriate level. With an expected eight-card fit (5 + 3) you raise to the eight-trick level and bid 2♠. With a nine-card fit (5 + 4) you raise to 3♠, and with a ten-card fit (5 + 5) you bid 4♠. With 10 points or more you will begin with a cue-bid in the opponent's suit.

Insight: Rebid by the overcaller

Suppose you have overcalled 1♠ and partner raises to 3♠. Remember that this is a weak bid! Partner would have cue-bid the opponent's suit with a good hand. So, do not raise to 4♠ simply because you have values to spare for your 1♠ overcall. Your partner has shown around six points and four-card support. You will need a good hand to make game opposite that.

After the start to the auction shown above, how would you respond on these South hands?

	a	b	c
♠	K 9 4	Q 10 7 2	A J 5
♥	10 5	8 4 3	A 8 2
♦	9 8 4 3	9 2	9 6
♣	Q 10 7 2	K J 8 4	Q 10 8 4 3

On hand **a** you raise partner's 1♠ overcall to 2♠. With hand **b**, and an expected nine-card fit, you raise pre-emptively to 3♠. Hand **c** represents a sound high-card raise to the two-level, almost to the three-level in this case, so you begin with a cue-bid of 2♦.

The cue-bid response to a take-out double

When you are responding to a take-out double you have two duties. You must choose a denomination (a trump suit or no-trumps). You must also give some idea of the strength of your hand, so that partner can judge if a game may be worth bidding. Suppose the auction starts like this:

West	North	East	South
–	1♣	Dble	Pass
?			

Sitting West, you would respond along these lines:

Pass	*Long and solid clubs – this is a rare action*
1♦/1♥/1♠	*About 0–7 points*
1NT	*6–10 points and a good club stopper*
2♦/2♥/2♠	*8–10 points*
2♣	*The cue-bid shows 11+ points*
2NT	*11–12 points and a good club stopper*
3NT	*13+ points and a good club stopper*
4♥/4♠	*With enough for game and a five-card suit*

So, you choose a trump suit at the minimum level when you hold a weak hand. With a hand of middle strength, about 8–10 points, you jump one level. When you hold upwards of 11 points but cannot tell which suit will be best, you show your general strength with a cue-bid in the enemy suit. Since this is the topic of the present section, let's see a couple of auctions that involve this particular response.

West	East	West	North	East	South
♠ K Q 8 3	♠ A J 9 2	–	–	–	1♣
♥ A J 8 2	♥ Q 3	Dble	Pass	2♣	Pass
♦ A J 6	♦ 9 5 4 2	2♥	Pass	2♠	Pass
♣ 9 3	♣ A 10 5	4♠			

East has the values to respond 2NT, but if there is a 4–4 spade fit he would like to play in that suit instead. He shows his general strength (11+ points) with a cue-bid and the two players bid their suits in ascending order until a fit is found. West shows his hearts and East shows his spades. If West were to raise to just 3♠ now, this would not be forcing. Since West holds 15 points and expects his partner to have 11 or more, he leaps to 4♠ and the best contract is reached.

West	East		West	North	East	South
♠ A Q 7 6	♠ K 9 8 4		–	–	–	3♦
♥ A J 2	♥ K 10 9 4		Dble	Pass	4♦	Pass
♦ A 5	♦ 9 6 3		4 ♠			
♣ J 8 6 4	♣ A 5					

East decides that his three good cards justify bidding to the game level. Should he bid 4♠ or 4♥, do you think? There is no need to guess! He shows his strength with a cue-bid of 4♦ and West will then bid his own suits up the line. In this case West does not hold four hearts and therefore rebids 4♠. Once again the best contract is reached.

Insight: Responding on a strong hand

Suppose partner doubles 1♥ and you have around 12–13 points and four spades. It is a common mistake to bid 2♠ on such a hand, but this shows only 8–10 points. Partner will often pass and you will have missed an easy game. One of the most important parts of bidding is to bid your games. With so many points, you should start with a bid in the opponent's suit.

POINTS TO REMEMBER

▶ *When you hold support for partner's suit and the auction becomes competitive, you should raise partner as high as is practical. On a hand with a moderate point-count, you will generally give a single raise when you have three-card support and a double raise with four-card support.*

▶ *Obviously, you cannot make the same bid with a weakish hand and a fairly strong hand. Any direct raises of partner's overcall tend to be pre-emptive in nature. When, instead, you have a sound game-try hand with 10 points or more, you indicate this with a cue-bid in the enemy suit.*

▶ *When you hold 11+ points opposite partner's take-out double, and no particularly long suit, you begin with a cue-bid. Both players then bid their suits upwards until a fit is found. The bidding may stop at the three-level if both players are minimum for their actions so far.*

TEST YOURSELF

1 *You are sitting East, and the bidding starts like this:*

West	North	East	South
1♥	2♦	?	

What will you bid on the following East hands?

a
♠ 8 5 3
♥ A 10 9 3 2
♦ 7
♣ Q 10 8 4

b
♠ 9 6 4
♥ J 8 4
♦ 10 8 6
♣ A K 9 4

c
♠ A Q 6
♥ K J 8 3
♦ 10 7
♣ J 9 3 2

2 *Now you are sitting South. The bidding starts like this:*

West	North	East	South
1♥	2♣	Pass	?

What will you bid on the following South hands?

a
♠ K 10 5 3
♥ 9 8 4 2
♦ J 5
♣ K 6 4

b
♠ A 9 6 4
♥ 10 3
♦ K J 6
♣ A 10 7 3

c
♠ K 8 4
♥ A J 9
♦ 10 9 7 2
♣ K 8 2

3 *Still in the South seat, you now face a take-out double from your partner. The bidding starts like this:*

West	North	East	South
1♥	Dble	Pass	?

How will you respond on the following South hands?

a
♠ A J 7 4
♥ 10 7 3
♦ K 2
♣ J 9 8 5

b
♠ K 8 2
♥ 9 8
♦ A Q J 6
♣ Q 10 7 2

c
♠ Q 3
♥ A Q 7 6
♦ 10 7 4
♣ K 9 8 2

(The answers are on page 200.)

11

··

Clues from the bidding

In this chapter you will learn:
- *how to make deductions from the enemy bidding*
- *when an opponent has opened 1NT*
- *when an opponent has pre-empted*
- *when an opponent has failed to open*
- *when an opponent has failed to respond.*

As declarer, you must gather information from every available
source. The opening lead, and the play to the first trick, will tell
you quite a bit about the lie of the suit that was led. Every time a
player shows out of a suit subsequently, it will help you to build
up a picture of the shape of the defenders' hands. You may also be
assisted by the signals that the defenders pass to each other. In this
chapter we will look at the clues provided by a fourth source – the
opponents' bidding or lack of it. Pay due attention in this area and
you can avoid many a guess in the play.

When an opponent has opened 1NT

It is particularly informative when an opponent opens 1NT, showing a balanced hand and a point-count within a narrow range. Look at this deal:

	♠ 9 8 5 3	
	♥ K J 6	
	♦ J 6 4	
	♣ A Q 7	
♠ J 7		♠ 6 2
♥ 9 8 4 2		♥ Q 7 5
♦ A K Q		♦ 10 9 5 2
♣ K 10 8 4		♣ 9 6 5 3
	♠ A K Q 10 4	
	♥ A 10 3	
	♦ 8 7 3	
	♣ J 2	

West	North	East	South
1NT	Pass	Pass	2♠
Pass	4♠	End	

West opens a weak 1NT, showing 12–14 points. You bid to 4♠ and West launches the defence by cashing the ace, king and queen of diamonds. How will you play the contract when West switches to the jack of trumps at Trick 2?

You win and draw trumps in one further round. The ♣J is covered by the king and ace and the contract is now yours if you can guess which defender holds the ♥Q. A lazy player might say to himself: 'West opened the bidding so I will finesse him for the missing queen.' A more disciplined declarer would note that West had already shown up with 9 points in diamonds, 1 point in trumps and 3 points in clubs. That is 13 points already and the ♥Q in addition would give him 15 points, too much for a weak 1NT opening. So, the correct play is to cross to the ♥K and then finesse the ♥10. East does indeed hold the ♥Q and you make the contract.

Suppose, instead, that West's 1NT opening had promised 15–17 points. Without the ♥Q he would hold only 14 points, so you would play the hand differently, finessing West for the ♥Q.

When an opponent has pre-empted

An opponent who pre-empts against you can prove a nuisance in the auction, robbing you of precious bidding space. If you end up playing the contract, however, the information provided by the pre-empt may be valuable in the play. Because the pre-empter is unusually long in his own suit, he will be correspondingly short in the other three suits. You will tend to finesse his partner for any missing honour. Look at this deal:

		♠ A J 8 6	
		♥ A Q 7	
		♦ K J 7 3	
		♣ A 10	
♠ 3			♠ Q 5 4
♥ 8 6 3			♥ 10 5 4 2
♦ 6 4			♦ Q 10 9 5
♣ K Q J 8 7 6 3			♣ 5 2
		♠ K 10 9 7 2	
		♥ K J 9	
		♦ A 8 2	
		♣ 9 4	

West	North	East	South
3♣	Dble	Pass	4♠
Pass	6♠	End	

North–South overbid somewhat, arriving in a poor slam. How would you play this contract when West leads the ♣K?

You win with the ♣A and see that your first task is to pick up the trump suit. Normally, with nine cards between the hands, you would play to drop a missing queen. The odds in favour of this play are only 52 per cent compared with 48 per cent, however, and these are easily overturned when you know that one of the defenders is particularly long in some other suit. Here you expect West to hold seven clubs to his partner's two. Since East will then hold eleven non-club cards to West's six, he is likely to be longer than West in each of the other three suits. In particular, the odds strongly favour finessing East for the missing ♠Q.

Insight: Missing four to the queen

When you have to decide whether to finesse against a missing queen or to play for the drop, the guideline is 'eight ever, nine never'. In other words, you should finesse with a total of eight cards and play for the drop with nine. The odds are extremely close with nine cards. If there is any reason (such as an overcall) to place a defender with longer trumps, you should finesse against him instead.

You cash the ♠A, finesse the ♠10 successfully and draw the last trump with the ♠K. You then play three rounds of hearts, both defenders following all the way. West has indicated seven clubs with his 3♣ opening and has shown up with one spade and at least three hearts. His shape is 1–3–2–7 (or 1–4–1–7) and he can hold no more than two cards in diamonds. When you play ace and another diamond, West follows with the ♦4 and the ♦6. There is no point taking a finesse of the ♦J because West cannot hold another diamond. You rise with the ♦K in dummy, leaving these cards still to be played:

Now you play dummy's ♣10. West has to win the trick and concede a ruff-and-discard with his return. You ruff in the dummy and discard your ♦8, making the slam.

Are you thinking: 'I could never make clever plays like that'? Yes, you can! When you take the trouble to count the defenders' hands, all sorts of plays become possible.

Remember that when a player is long in one suit (perhaps he has pre-empted or overcalled), he is likely to be shorter than his partner in the other three suits. This will often affect the way that you play those suits.

When an opponent has failed to open

A player who had the chance to open the bidding but declined to do so will generally hold fewer than 12 points. If he has shown up with, say, 10 points in three suits, he is unlikely to hold the queen of the fourth suit. Inferences of this sort will often allow you to place the cards successfully. Test yourself on this deal:

```
              ♠ 9 5 2
              ♥ 9 7 2
              ♦ K J 4 2
              ♣ K 10 4
 ♠ K Q J 7         N         ♠ 10 6 4 3
 ♥ Q J 8      W         E    ♥ 6
 ♦ Q 9 6                     ♦ A 10 7 3
 ♣ 9 7 5           S         ♣ J 8 3 2
              ♠ A 8
              ♥ A K 10 5 4 3
              ♦ 8 5
              ♣ A Q 6
```

West	North	East	South
Pass	Pass	Pass	1♥
Pass	2♥	Pass	4♥
End			

West leads the ♠K against your game in hearts. You win with the ace and cash the ace and king of trumps, discovering that West began with Q-J-8 in the suit. With two certain losers in the major suits, you will now need to guess how to play the diamonds. How will you continue?

West's lead of the ♠K more or less guarantees that he also holds the ♠Q, quite possibly the ♠J as well. Since he has also shown up with ♥Q-J-x, he began with 8 or 9 points in the major suits. The ♦A in addition would have given him an opening bid of some sort, so you can place this card with East. The only chance is that West holds the ♦Q, which would leave him with 10 or 11 points, just short of an opening bid. You therefore play a diamond to the jack. This does indeed force the ace, as you were hoping, and the contract is yours.

When an opponent has failed to respond

A player who holds upwards of 6 points will generally respond to an opening one-bid in a suit. The fact that a player did not find such a response will severely limit the points that he can hold. Take the South cards on this deal:

West	North	East	South
1♣	Pass	Pass	1♠
Pass	2♣	Pass	2♦
Pass	4♠	End	

West leads the ♣A against your spade game and switches to the ♥Q at Trick 2. East wins dummy's ♥K with the ace and returns a heart to West's ten. How will you play the contract when West persists with the ♥J at Trick 4?

You ruff in the South hand and must now pick up the trump suit to make the contract. With eight cards between the hands you would normally finesse East for the missing ♠Q, crossing to the ♠A and finessing the ♠J on the second round. Here, however, East has already shown up with the ♥A and he failed to find a response to partner's 1♣ opening. It is reasonable to deduce that West holds the ♠Q. You therefore play the ♠A and ♠K, claiming your reward when the queen falls doubleton offside.

Insight: Other inferences

We have been considering high-card points here but you can also make deductions about suit lengths. Suppose the opponents start 1♦ – 1NT. You can assume that responder has no four-card major. Suppose that they bid 1♠ – 2♦ – 2♠, you can deduce that the opener is unlikely to hold four hearts. Whether playing the contract or defending, think back to the bidding.

Suppose, instead, that East had made some low-level response. You would then be inclined to place East with 6 points and would have no reason not to finesse him for the ♠Q.

Deductions from a bid that was not made

When you are defending, your task is often lightened by clues from the other side's bidding. Take the East cards here and see if you would have beaten 4♠.

♠ J 10 4 3
♥ Q J 3
♦ A 7
♣ Q 10 8 5

♠ A 8 2
♥ 9 2
♦ J 8 6 5 2
♣ K 9 2

♠ 9 7
♥ A 10 7 6 4
♦ Q 9 3
♣ 7 4 3

♠ K Q 6 5
♥ K 8 5
♦ K 10 4
♣ A J 6

West	North	East	South
–	–	–	1NT
Pass	2♣	Pass	2♠
Pass	4♠	End	

Your partner (West) leads the ♥9 against South's spade game. What is your plan for the defence?

The ♥9 would not be led from ♥9-x-x or ♥9-x-x-x, so it is either a singleton or top of a doubleton. If the lead is a singleton, you should win with the ace and deliver a ruff immediately. If instead the lead is from a doubleton, you must duck the first round. The hope then is that West will gain the lead with the ace or king of trumps and will be able to cross to your ♥A for a third-round ruff. Which is it to be?

To determine the answer, you must think back to the bidding. If South held four hearts, as well as four spades, he would have responded 2♥ to North's Stayman enquiry. In the absence of such a response he must hold three hearts, leaving West with a doubleton. You play an encouraging ♥10 on the first round and declarer then plays a trump. West wins with the trump ace and plays his second heart to your ace. A heart ruff gives the defence their third trick and the ♦K will then put the game one down.

POINTS TO REMEMBER

▶ *When you are trying to place honour cards in the defenders'*
  hands, remember any evidence provided by the auction.
  A defender who opened the bidding will usually hold
  12 points or more. A defender who responded will usually
  hold at least 6 points.

▶ *Particularly informative bids are 1NT openings and*
  pre-emptive openings that indicate a seven-card suit.

▶ *Remember also the bids that were not made and the inferences*
  that follow. A player who did not open, for example, will
  usually hold fewer then 12 points. A player who failed to
  respond to a one-bid will usually hold fewer than 6 points.

▶ *By playing on the other three suits, to discover the defenders'*
  length and high-card points there, you may find it easier to
  read the lie of the fourth suit.

TEST YOURSELF

1

♠ Q 5 4 2
♥ 9 7 2
♦ A Q 4
♣ K J 4

♥K led

♠ K 10 9 8 6 3
♥ A 5
♦ K J 5
♣ 6 3

West	North	East	South
1NT	Pass	Pass	2♠
Pass	4♠	End	

West opens a 12–14 point 1NT and you end in 4♠. How will you play this contract when West leads the ♥K?

(The answer is on page 201.)

2

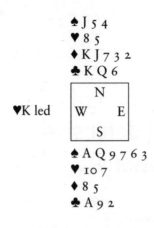

♠ J 5 4
♥ 8 5
♦ K J 7 3 2
♣ K Q 6

♥K led

N
W   E
S

♠ A Q 9 7 6 3
♥ 10 7
♦ 8 5
♣ A 9 2

West	North	East	South
3♥	Pass	Pass	3♠
Pass	4♠	End	

West leads the ♥K, East overtaking with the ♥A and returning a second round of hearts to the ten and jack. How will you play the contract when West then switches to the ♣7?

(The answer is on page 202.)

12

Maintaining defensive communications

In this chapter you will learn:
- *how to keep in touch with partner in defence*
- *when to hold up a high card in defence*
- *about ducking when partner leads your suit*
- *how to take stoppers in the right order.*

Just as declarer has to manage communications between his own hand and the dummy, so do the defenders have to take steps to keep in touch with each other. The most important situation is when you have led a long suit against a no-trump contract and want to be able cash your winners, once the suit has been established.

Returning the right card

To enable the opening leader to read the lie of the suit, his partner must follow an agreed procedure when choosing which card to return on the second round. Look at this deal:

♠ 6 5 2
♥ 7 6
♦ 10 9 3 2
♣ K Q 5 3

♠ Q 10 8 4
♥ A 10 8 5 2
♦ 8 4
♣ 10 7

N
W   E
S

♠ J 7
♥ K 9 3
♦ A 7 5
♣ J 8 6 4 2

♠ A K 9 3
♥ Q J 4
♦ K Q J 6
♣ A 9

West	North	East	South
–	–	–	2NT
Pass	3NT	End	

Sitting West, you lead the ♥5 against 3NT. Your partner wins with the ♥K and returns the ♥9, covered by declarer's ♥Q. What will you do on this trick?

Let's see first what will happen if you win with the ♥A and play a third round of hearts to clear the suit. Declarer will win with the ♥J and play on diamonds. When your partner wins with the ♦A, he will have no heart to return. Declarer will capture East's return in some other suit and score nine tricks.

What went wrong? By capturing the second round of hearts with the ace, you lost touch with your partner. The winning defence was to play low on the second round of hearts, allowing South's ♥Q to win. When your partner subsequently took his ♦A he would have a heart to return. You would win this third round of hearts with the ace and cash two more heart winners to put 3NT one down.

If declarer had started with ♥Q-4 (instead of ♥Q-J-4) it would not be a good idea to allow him to win the second round, of course! So, you need to know what cards declarer holds in the suit. Your partner will help you to read the lie of the cards by following this rule with his lead to the second round of the suit:

When you have two cards remaining, return the higher one.

With more than two, return the original fourth-best card.

Look back to the deal on the previous page. East returned the ♥9. This told you that he had started with ♥K-9-3 (or ♥K-9 doubleton). When East has ♥K-9-3, declarer has a certain trick with his ♥Q-J-4. It is essential to duck the second round of the suit to allow your partner to cross to your ♥A later. (When partner holds a doubleton heart it is unlikely to make any difference, whatever you do.)

Let's see a deal where it would be wrong to hold up. Remember the rule above and see if you would have been able to tell, sitting West, whether to hold up your high card or not.

	♠ 8 6		
	♥ Q 7 2		
	♦ Q J 9 3		
	♣ A Q 5 3		

♠ A 10 7 5 4   ♠ K J 3 2
♥ 9 8 5 3   ♥ A 10 4
♦ 7 5   ♦ 10 4 2
♣ 7 4   ♣ 9 8 6

♠ Q 9
♥ K J 6
♦ A K 8 6
♣ K J 10 2

West	North	East	South
–	–	–	1NT
Pass	3NT	End	

You lead the ♠5 and East wins with the ♠K, South following with the ♠9. East returns the ♠2 and declarer plays the ♠Q. Will you hold up or not?

East's ♠2 return looks like an original fourth-best card. In that case, declarer began with ♠Q-9 doubleton, and you must take your ace immediately. (If you don't, in fact, declarer will score eight more tricks in the minor suits and make the contract.) The only other possibility is that East began with ♠K-2 and that declarer holds ♠Q-J-9-3. In that case, your play is unlikely to make any difference. So, you should win with the ♠A and return the ♠4. The defenders will score five spade tricks and the ♥A, putting the game two down.

Was declarer more likely to hold ♠Q-9, or ♠Q-J-9-3, do you think? He was almost certain to hold the doubleton combination! Otherwise he would have no reason to waste his ♠9 at Trick 1. He would have followed with the ♠3 instead.

So, look carefully at the card that partner returns. You will often be able to work out how the suit lies and whether it is right for you to hold up your high card.

Ducking when your suit is led

One of the main reasons for bidding a good suit is that you want partner to lead it if the opponents win the auction. Suppose you overcall 1♠ on ♠A-K-J-10-5 and the player on your left becomes declarer in 3NT. Your partner leads the ♠8 and you may now have to take special steps to keep in touch with him. Let's put that spade suit into a complete deal:

```
                    ♠ 7 4 2
                    ♥ A 8 3
                    ♦ K Q 4
                    ♣ A K Q 10
      ♠ 8 6             N          ♠ A K J 10 5
      ♥ J 7 5 2                    ♥ Q 10 6
      ♦ A 9 7 3    W       E       ♦ 8 6 2
      ♣ 7 6 3          S          ♣ 8 5
                    ♠ Q 9 3
                    ♥ K 9 4
                    ♦ J 10 5
                    ♣ J 9 4 2
```

West	North	East	South
–	1♣	1♠	1NT
Pass	3NT	End	

You overcall 1♠ and your partner leads the ♠8 against the eventual 3NT contract. How will you defend in the East seat?

It may seem natural to win with the ♠K and to clear the spade suit by continuing with the ♠A and ♠J, forcing out South's ♠Q. This defence will not beat the contract, however. With only seven tricks on top, declarer will have to set up two tricks in diamonds. When your partner wins with the ♦A he will have no spade to return! Declarer will capture whatever other suit West returns and score nine tricks for his contract.

To keep in touch with partner you must not play the king or ace of spades on the first trick. You should play the ♠10 instead, letting South score his spade trick at a moment that suits you. Do you see the point of defending in this way? You leave your partner with a spade in his hand. When declarer eventually plays on diamonds, your partner will rise immediately with the ♦A and return his remaining spade. The defenders will score four spade tricks and one diamond trick to beat the contract.

Insight: Holding up an ace

Another situation when you might duck arises in a suit contract. Suppose you hold ♦A 10 6 4 and your partner leads the ♦9. If you read this is as a doubleton rather than a singleton (perhaps because of the bidding), you would duck the first round. When partner gained the lead subsequently, maybe with a top trump, he could cross to your ♦A for a diamond ruff.

Sometimes you would make this ducking play even with the ace-king-queen in your suit. Suppose you have overcalled 1♠ and South is now in 3NT with the spade suit lying like this:

                          North
                          ♠ 8 4
West   East
♠ 7 2   ♠ A K Q 10 5
                          South
                          ♠ J 9 6 3

Partner leads the ♠7. It is fairly obvious that South must hold a
spade stopper, in order to justify his no-trump bid. Play the ♠10
and let him win his spade trick immediately. Then your partner will
have a spade to return if he gains the lead.

Taking stoppers in the right order

Sometimes declarer has two stoppers to knock out, before he can
score the nine tricks that he needs for 3NT. This will give you more
time, as defenders, to establish your own suit. It may be important,
though, that you take your stoppers in the right order. You will
want to leave an entry to the hand with the long cards in the
defenders' suit. This deal illustrates the situation:

                          ♠ K 4
                          ♥ A 8 3
                          ♦ 10 9 4 3
                          ♣ K J 9 4
♠ Q J 10 7 3   N   ♠ 9 8 6
♥ J 7 5 2   ♥ Q 10 6
♦ K 5   W   E   ♦ A 6 2
♣ 7 6   S   ♣ 10 8 5 3
                          ♠ A 5 2
                          ♥ K 9 4
                          ♦ Q J 8 7
                          ♣ A Q 5

West	North	East	South
–	–	–	1NT (15–17)
Pass	3NT	End	

West, your partner, leads the ♠Q against 3NT. Declarer can count eight top tricks and sees that he will have to set up the diamond suit in order to score a ninth trick. Correctly, he allows the ♠Q to win the first trick and wins the next round of spades with dummy's king. (If spades had been 6–2 between the defenders' hands, declarer's hold-up would have left East with no spade to play.)

Now comes the key moment for the defence. Declarer leads the ♦3 from dummy. How will you defend in the East seat?

To beat the contract, you must rise immediately with the ♦A and return your remaining spade. This will clear the spade suit and partner will then have two spade tricks to cash when he wins the next round of diamonds with the king. Suppose you are not awake and play low on the first round of diamonds. Your partner wins with the ♦K and clears the spade suit but he will never gain the lead to cash his two winners. When you win the next round of diamonds with the ace, you will have no spade to play.

Some players are worried about rising with the ♦A on deals like this, in case declarer holds ♦K-J-x-x and has a guess to make in the suit. That's possible, but you still won't beat the contract by playing low on the first round of diamonds. Say that declarer plays the ♦J to partner's ♦Q and the spades are cleared. Again you will have no spade to play when you win with the ♦A.

POINTS TO REMEMBER

▶ *When you are returning the suit that partner has led, lead the top card when you have two cards remaining and the original fourth best from any longer holding.*

▶ *When you have led from a long suit headed by an honour, it may be right to hold up the high card on the second round. By leaving partner with a card in the suit, you will benefit if he gains the lead later and can cross to your high card. You will then be able to cash your established winners.*

▶ *When the defenders hold two stoppers in declarer's suits it may be important to take them in the right order. You will want to preserve the high card that will serve as an entry to the long cards in the defenders' main suit.*

TEST YOURSELF

1

```
              ♠ A 7 6 4
              ♥ Q 7
              ♦ A K 5
              ♣ 9 8 7 2
♠ Q 8 2           N
♥ A 10 8 5 3    W   E
♦ 8 7 4           S
♣ 6 4
```

West	North	East	South
–	–	–	1♣
Pass	1♠	Pass	1NT (12–14)
Pass	3NT	End	

Sitting West, you lead the ♥5. The ♥7 is played from dummy, covered by East's ♥9 and declarer's ♥K. Declarer crosses to the ♦A and leads the ♣2. East wins with the ♣K and returns the ♥6, South playing the ♥4. How will you defend from this point?

2

```
              ♠ Q J 7
              ♥ J 5
              ♦ A K Q J 5
              ♣ 7 5 2
♥8 led            N          ♠ 8 5 2
                W   E        ♥ A K 9 7 3 2
                  S          ♦ 8 2
                             ♣ Q 8
```

West	North	East	South
–	1♦	1♥	2NT
Pass	3NT	End	

Your partner, West, leads the ♥8 against 3NT and the ♥J is played from dummy. What is your plan for the defence?

(The answers are on page 203.)

13

Playing a cross-ruff

In this chapter you will learn:
- *how to play a cross-ruff*
- *to cash side-suit winners before the cross-ruff*.

When you are playing in a suit contract, it is quite common to take a ruff or two in the dummy and then to draw trumps in your hand. In this chapter we will look at a slightly unusual way of playing a contract. When you have a side-suit shortage in your own hand as well as in the dummy, it may be best to take ruffs in both hands. This style of play is known as a cross-ruff. You never actually draw trumps and the defenders will usually end up with more trumps than you!

How to play a cross-ruff

Let's see an example of this style of play straight away.

```
              ♠ A Q 10 2
              ♥ A 9 5 4 2
              ♦ 7 6 4
              ♣ 7
♠ 8 7                          ♠ 6 5 3
♥ Q 6          N              ♥ K J 10 7 3
♦ K J 5 2    W   E           ♦ Q 10
♣ Q 10 9 8 4   S              ♣ K 5 3
              ♠ K J 9 4
              ♥ 8
              ♦ A 9 8 3
              ♣ A J 6 2
```

West	North	East	South
–	–	–	1♣
Pass	1♥	Pass	1♠
Pass	3♠	Pass	4♠
End			

West leads the ♠8 against your spade game. How will you play the contract?

You have only three winners in the side suits (the three aces). If you can add seven trump tricks, this will bring your total to ten. You win the first trick with the ♠A in dummy and must now aim to score all six of your remaining trumps separately. You cash the ♥A and ruff a heart with the ♠9. You then play the ♦A, scoring the one diamond trick that you need, and continue with the ♣A. Next you ruff a club with dummy's only low trump, the ♠2, which gives you six tricks in the bag. A heart ruff with the jack is followed by a club ruff with the queen, a heart ruff with the king and a final club ruff with the ace. Since the last four ruffs were taken with master trumps, there was no risk of an overruff by the defenders. Ten tricks are duly made and the game is yours.

Insight: High cross-ruff

When a declarer claims a contract, you may hear him say: 'I will make the rest on a high cross-ruff'. This means that each ruff will be taken with a master trump, so there will be no possibility of an overruff. This is why you should take the early ruffs with low trumps, so that you will eventually have a high cross-ruff for the contract.

One point to remember is that you will normally ruff with low trumps at the start of the hand, when the risk of an overruff is minimal. Later in the hand, you can ruff with master trumps and will not need to worry if a defender is out of the suit being ruffed.

Cashing side-suit winners before the cross-ruff

On many cross-ruff deals it is essential to cash all your side-suit winners before embarking on the ruffing. If you fail to do so, the defenders may discard their cards in one of the suits and then ruff your winners. It's not easy to visualize, perhaps, so let's see a deal that illustrates the situation.

```
              ♠ 2
              ♥ Q J 9 3
              ♦ K 7 5
              ♣ A J 7 5 2
  ♠ 6 3          N          ♠ K Q 10 9 5
  ♥ 10 6 4 2  W     E       ♥ 7
  ♦ 9 8          S          ♦ Q J 4 3 2
  ♣ K Q 10 8 4              ♣ 6 3
              ♠ A J 8 7 4
              ♥ A K 8 5
              ♦ A 10 6
              ♣ 9
```

West	North	East	South
–	–	–	1♠
Pass	2♣	Pass	2♥
Pass	4♥	Pass	6♥
End			

South's final bid was somewhat exuberant, it's true, but how would you play the heart slam when West leads the ♣K?

You have four winners in the side suits. If you can add eight trump tricks, by ruffing four spades in the dummy and four clubs in your hand, this will bring the total to 12. Suppose you win the club lead with dummy's ace and begin to cross-ruff in the black suits immediately. When you lead the third round of spades, West will take the opportunity to discard one of his diamonds. You will go down! You will not be able to score the two diamond tricks that you need.

After winning the club lead, the first thing you should do is to cash the ace and king of diamonds ('before the rats get at them', as bridge players say). That done, you play the ♠A and ruff a spade with the ♥3. You then ruff a club in your hand with the ♥5. As before, you are taking the early ruffs with low trumps, while the risk of an overruff is minimal.

When you lead another spade, West has no cards left in the suit. He cannot make a damaging discard of a diamond, as before, because you have already cashed your two diamond tricks. It won't help him to ruff, since you would overruff in the dummy, so he will doubtless throw a club. You ruff with dummy's ♥9 and ruff another club with the ♥8 as East shows out. The contract is now yours. Dummy has the ♥Q-J remaining and you have the ♥A-K. You make these master trumps separately by continuing to cross-ruff the two black suits. Twelve tricks are soon before you.

POINTS TO REMEMBER

▶ *When you have a side-suit shortage in both hands the best play may be a cross-ruff. You plan to score the trumps in both hands separately, by taking ruffs in two suits.*

▶ *When playing a cross-ruff you should usually score the early ruffs with low trumps, when the risk of an overruff is minimal. The later ruffs can then be taken with higher trumps, perhaps master trumps.*

▶ *Before embarking on a cross-ruff, you should cash the side-suit winners that you need. If you fail to do this, the defenders may discard as you cross-ruff and later be in a position to ruff your intended side-suit winners.*

TEST YOURSELF

1

♠ K 9 7 3
♥ J 10 9 5
♦ A 9 7 4
♣ 7

♦Q led

♠ A 5 4
♥ A K Q 4
♦ 3
♣ J 10 5 3 2

West	North	East	South
–	–	–	1♣
Pass	1♦	Pass	1♥
Pass	3♥	Pass	4♥
End			

West leads the ♦Q. How will you play the heart game?

(The answer is on page 205.)

2

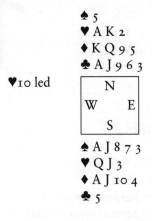

♠ 5
♥ A K 2
♦ K Q 9 5
♣ A J 9 6 3

♥10 led

♠ A J 8 7 3
♥ Q J 3
♦ A J 10 4
♣ 5

West	North	East	South
–	–	–	1♠
Pass	2♣	Pass	2♦
Pass	4NT	Pass	5♥
Pass	6♦	End	

West leads the ♥10 against your small slam. How will you plan the play?

(The answer is on page 206.)

....

Transfer responses

In this chapter you will learn:
- *transfer responses when partner opens 1NT*
- *transfer responses when partner overcalls 1NT*
- *transfer responses when partner opens 2NT*
- *when you should 'break the transfer'.*

Nearly all tournament players use 'transfer responses' when partner has opened 1NT. What does that mean?

> **Transfer responses to 1NT**
>
> 2♦ *shows at least five hearts and asks opener to rebid 2♥.*
>
> 2♥ *shows at least five spades and asks opener to rebid 2♠.*

What is the point of such a method? There are two big advantages. The first is that the 1NT opener will be able to play any contract in responder's five-card major. His hand will be hidden from view and his honour holdings will be protected from the opening lead. The second advantage is that after a start of 1NT – 2♦ – 2♥, responder has a second chance to bid. He can continue with a further bid, such as 2NT, 3♣ or 3NT, having already shown five hearts.

(The examples in this chapter will assume that a 12–14 point weak 1NT is being used. If your preference is to use the 15–17 point strong 1NT, this will not affect the meaning of any of the sequences at all. You should just mentally add a king to the opening bidder's hand and subtract a king from the responder's hand.)

So, let's see some examples of transfer bids in action. The first situation is where responder is weak and wants to sign off in his long major suit.

West	East	West	East
♠ A 9 3 2	♠ 7 4	1NT	2♦
♥ K 5 2	♥ A J 8 4 3	2♥	
♦ Q J 7	♦ 10 6 5		
♣ K 10 4	♣ Q 8 2		

If transfer bids were not being used, East would have signed off in 2♥ and played the contract himself. Playing transfers, he responds 2♦ instead. The opener rebids 2♥, as requested, and East passes. Note that West's 2♥ bid does not indicate three-card heart support. He would have to make the same rebid even if he held only two hearts.

Since bidding 2♦ forces the opener to rebid 2♥, the responder has the chance to give a second description of his hand. For example, if he continues with 2NT this will show the values to invite game:

West	East	West	East
♠ K 2	♠ J 8 4	1NT	2♦
♥ A 10 4	♥ K Q 8 6 5	2♥	2NT
♦ Q 9 8 3	♦ A J 5	4♥	
♣ K Q 6 3	♣ 10 2		

East's sequence passes two messages to his partner: a) 'I have five hearts' and b) 'I am strong enough to invite game but not to insist on it'. West can now place the final contract. With a minimum 1NT opening, he would pass 2NT (with only two hearts) or sign off in 3♥ (with three hearts). With two hearts and a maximum opening, he would raise to 3NT. With four hearts, or three hearts and a maximum opening, he would bid 4♥.

Suppose East had held the ♠A instead of the ♠J on that last hand. What would he have rebid? He would have said 3NT at his second turn, asking partner to choose between 3NT and 4♥.

With six trumps and game-try values, responder can rebid in the trump suit:

West	East	West	East
♠ 9 2	♠ K Q 8 7 6 3	1NT	2♥
♥ K J 7 3	♥ A 5	2♠	3♠
♦ A 10 7	♦ J 6 3		
♣ K J 9 5	♣ 8 2		

East shows six spades and the values to invite a game. West has only two low spades and a minimum 12-count, so he declines the invitation.

Insight: Four-suit transfers

It is beyond the scope of this book but some tournament players use 'four-suit transfers'. As well as the 2♦ and 2♥ transfers that we have seen, they use 2♠ as a transfer to show clubs and 2NT to show diamonds. On a hand that would otherwise be shown by a limit-bid response of 2NT, they have to bid a Stayman 2♣ and then 2NT.

When the responder has the values for game, at least, he may bid a new suit on the second round:

West	East	West	East
♠ 8 2	♠ A Q 9 7 2	1NT	2♥
♥ A Q 7	♥ K 5	2♠	3♦
♦ K J 9 3	♦ A Q 10 4	4♦	6♦
♣ Q J 9 5	♣ A 7		

East shows five spades and (at least) four diamonds, with game-forcing values. West raises the diamonds and East bids a small slam in that suit. Suppose, instead, that East held the same shape but only 13 points. If there were no spade fit, he would rather play in no-trumps than diamonds. It follows that he should not even offer the diamond suit. He should rebid 3NT at his second turn, asking partner to choose between spades and no-trumps.

Transfers opposite a 1NT overcall

When partner has overcalled 1NT, it is a good idea to use exactly the same conventional responses (Stayman and transfer bids) as you would opposite a 1NT opening.

West	East	West	North	East	South
♠ A Q 9	♠ 4 3	–	–	–	1♠
♥ Q 7	♥ K 10 9 7 2	1NT	Pass	2♦	Pass
♦ K J 8 2	♦ A 9 3	2♥	Pass	3NT	
♣ A 10 6 4	♣ K 7 3				

East shows a five-card heart suit and the values for game. Since West has only two-card heart support, he opts to pass 3NT.

Transfers opposite a 2NT opening

A similar method is used opposite an opening bid of 2NT (or when the bidding has started 2♣ – 2♦ – 2NT):

Transfer responses to 2NT

3♦ shows at least five hearts and asks opener to rebid 3♥.

3♥ shows at least five spades and asks opener to rebid 3♠.

The advantages are the same as before. The opener will play the contract, with his values hidden from view and his tenaces protected from the opening lead. Also, responder will have the chance to make a second descriptive bid. Look at this typical sequence:

West	East	West	North	East	South
♠ A Q 7	♠ J 9 6 5 2	2NT	Pass	3♥	Pass
♥ A 7	♥ 8 5 4	3♠	Pass	3NT	Pass
♦ K Q 9 4	♦ A J 3	4♠			
♣ K Q J 3	♣ 9 5				

East shows a five-card spade suit with his transfer response and continues with 3NT to offer the opener a choice of game contracts. With three-card spade support, the opener chooses to play in partner's suit.

Breaking the transfer

When the opener has four-card trump support and an upper-range hand, he should bid one level higher than normal. This is known as 'breaking the transfer'. One advantage is that game may now be reached when responder was not quite strong enough to make a try himself. That's what happens here:

West	East	West	East
♠ Q 10 7 3	♠ J 4	1NT	2♦
♥ A 8 5 2	♥ K Q 9 7 3	3♥	4♥
♦ K 2	♦ A 9 6 4		
♣ A J 4	♣ 7 5		

With just 10 points and a five-card suit, East would have passed a rebid of 2♥. When partner shows four-card heart support and an upper-range opening, East raises to game.

Similarly, the knowledge that partner has a particularly good fit for your major suit may help you to bid a slam.

Other responses to 1NT

Some tournament players use 2♠ as a transfer response showing
five clubs and 2NT as transfer response showing five diamonds.
That is beyond the scope of this book. For the moment, it is best to
start with a Stayman response on strong hands that contain a five-
card minor. You can then bid the minor on the second round. Such
a rebid is forcing to game.

West	East	West	East
♠ A J 8 5	♠ Q 4	1NT	2♣
♥ J 10 6	♥ A K 7 5	2♠	3♣
♦ A Q 4	♦ K 3	3NT	
♣ 9 7 2	♣ K Q 10 8 3		

You begin with 2♣, hoping to uncover a heart fit. When partner
denies a heart fit by responding 2♠, you continue with the natural
and forcing 3♣, showing at least five clubs. West has no special fit
for clubs, so he signs off in 3NT and you have no more to say.

An immediate jump response at the three-level shows at least a
six-card suit and the possibility of a slam. When the opener's hand
is suitable for a slam, he should indicate this by making a cue-bid
(showing where he holds an ace or king).

West	East	West	East
♠ A 8 7 5	♠ K 4	1NT	3♥
♥ K 10 6	♥ A Q J 9 8 3	3♠	4NT
♦ A 9 6 2	♦ K 7	5♣	6♥
♣ Q 2	♣ K J 8		

East shows a six-card heart suit and suggests a slam. With three-
card heart support, a ruffing value and some useful honour cards,
West accepts the try by cue-bidding his ♠A. East bids Roman
Key-card Blackwood and the excellent small slam is reached.

POINTS TO REMEMBER

▶ In tournament play, most players use transfer responses to 1NT openings and overcalls. A 2♦ response shows five hearts and asks the opener to rebid 2♥. A 2♥ response shows five spades and the opener should rebid 2♠.

▶ Responder may follow his transfer bid with a further descriptive bid on the next round.

▶ Transfer bids are also used opposite a 2NT opening (or after a start of 2♣ – 2♦ – 2NT).

▶ With four-card support and maximum for his bid, the opener may 'break the transfer' by rebidding one level higher than normal.

TEST YOURSELF

1 *You are playing Stayman and transfers and your partner has opened a 12–14 point 1NT. What is your bidding plan, as responder, on the following hands?*

a ♠ Q 10 8 3 2   b ♠ K 3   c ♠ A K 10 8 6
  ♥ 9 2   ♥ A Q J 7 4   ♥ 5
  ♦ K 5 3   ♦ 10 8   ♦ A K J 2
  ♣ A 6 2   ♣ Q J 4 3   ♣ K 8 4

2 *Again your partner has opened a 12–14 point 1NT. What is your bidding plan on these responding hands?*

a ♠ 3   b ♠ K J 9 3   c ♠ 9 6
  ♥ A J 8 2   ♥ 8 4   ♥ A Q J 9 6 2
  ♦ K Q 3   ♦ A Q 10 7 6   ♦ 10 7
  ♣ A K 6 4 2   ♣ Q 7   ♣ A 8 2

3 *Your partner opens 2NT, showing 20–22 points. What is your bidding plan on these responding hands?*

a ♠ 7   b ♠ Q J 9 3 2   c ♠ 9 8 6
  ♥ K 10 8 2   ♥ 10 8 4   ♥ Q 9 6 5 2
  ♦ Q 6 2   ♦ K 8 7 2   ♦ 10 7 4 2
  ♣ A Q J 4 2   ♣ 7   ♣ 8

(The answers are on page 207.)

15

Safety plays

In this chapter you will learn:
- *how to calculate the best play in a suit*
- *how the best play may vary according to the tricks needed*
- *when you should avoid the 'normal play'*
- *how the best play may vary according to the lie of other suits.*

What does the term 'safety play' mean? Depending on the context it can have various meanings. It can mean, 'a way of playing the contract that guarantees its success'. This is also called a '100 per cent safety play'. It can also mean 'the way of playing a contract that will give you the best chance of making it'. Finally, the term can simply mean 'the best way to play a particular suit'. As we will see shortly, this may well depend on the number of tricks that you need from the suit. In this chapter we will see examples of all these meanings.

Safety plays in a single suit

Let's look first at the play of a single suit, with various honour combinations in the two hands. What do you think is the best way to play this diamond suit?

North
♦ K J 7 5

South
♦ A 6 2

The correct answer is, 'It depends on how many tricks I need from the suit!' Suppose you need four diamond tricks to make the contract. This can be done only when West holds ♦Q-x-x. You play the ♦A on the first round and finesse the ♦J on the second round. When the perfect lie does occur, the finesse will win and the ♦K will drop West's ♦Q on the third round. You will have your four tricks from the suit.

Next, suppose that you need only three diamond tricks to make the contract. How should you play the suit then? If you follow the same line (♦A first and then finesse the ♦J), you will make at least three tricks in these three cases:

a   when West holds the ♦Q

b   when diamonds break 3–3

c   when East holds a singleton ♦Q

A better play, when aiming for three tricks, is to cash the ♦K and ♦A and then to lead towards the ♦J. You will still succeed in cases **a, b** and **c** but you will add:

d   when East holds a doubleton ♦Q

When only three diamond tricks are needed to make the contract, you should follow this second line. By doing so, you will give yourself the best possible chance of making the contract. You give up the chance for four diamond tricks, yes, but an overtrick is not worth very much. You must always maximize your chance of making the contract. A bridge player would say: 'The safety play for three diamond tricks is to cash the king and ace and then lead towards the jack.'

There are many suit combinations that offer you the chance of making a safety play. Before we consider the general question of how you can work out the best plays for yourself, let's see a few more suit combinations.

```
                    North
                    ♣ K J 7 5
      West                          East
      ♣ Q                           ♣ 10 8 6 3
                    South
                    ♣ A 9 4 2
```

When you need four club tricks from this North–South combination, you should begin with a low club from the South hand, intending to finesse dummy's jack. You will score four tricks when West holds ♣Q, ♣Q-x or ♣Q-x-x. Note that it would not be correct to cash the ♣A on the first round, before finessing the ♣J. You would then fail to score four tricks when West held a singleton ♣Q. By leading low on the first round, you can win West's singleton ♣Q with the ♣K, continue with the ♣J and finesse the ♣9 on the third round.

How would you play the same combination if you needed only three club tricks?

```
                    North
                    ♣ K J 7 5
      West                          East
      ♣ 10 8 6 3                    ♣ Q
                    South
                    ♣ A 9 4 2
```

If you make the same play that is recommended when seeking four club tricks (low to the ♣J on the first round), you would score only two club tricks when the suit lies as in this second diagram. The safety play for three club tricks (a 100% safety play, in fact) is to cash the ♣K on the first round and to lead towards the South hand, intending to finesse the ♣9 on the second round. When East holds

♣Q-10-8-x, you will score three club tricks, whether or not East decides to play the 10 on the second round. If, instead, West held ♣Q-10-8-x, East would show out on the second round. You would rise with the ♣A and lead back towards the ♣J on the third round, again making the three tricks you required.

It may all seem a bit complicated, the first time you study a particular combination like this. When you have played bridge for a while, such holdings become familiar and you can easily remember the correct play.

Insight: Safety plays in a duplicate pairs

Many safety plays aim to give you the best chance of making a contract at IMPs. When these involve surrendering the best chance of an overtrick, they are not necessarily correct at duplicate pairs. To score only +600 for nine tricks at 3NT could give you a near-bottom score when others score +630. So, at pairs you often have to risk your contract to seek an overtrick!

Many safety plays involve testing for a key defensive honour to fall before taking a finesse (as we saw with our first example, A-x-x opposite K-J-x-x). Here is another one:

North
♦ A Q 6 2

South
♦ 7 5 4

To make 3NT, let's say, you need just two diamond tricks. You have adequate protection in the other suits, so you can choose your play in diamonds. Suppose you give the matter little thought and finesse the ♦Q on the first round. You will make the required two diamond tricks in just two situations:

a when West holds the ♦K

b when diamonds break 3–3

Can you see a better way to play the combination? You must try to make two tricks in a third situation, when East holds a doubleton ♦K. Suppose the suit lies like this:

                        North
                        ♦ A Q 6 2
        West   *East*
        ♦ J 9 8 3   ♦ K 10
                        South
                        ♦ 7 5 4

If you finesse on the first round, you will make only one diamond trick. The correct safety play for two tricks is to duck the first round, play the ace on the second round and then lead towards the queen on the third round. You still make two tricks in cases **a** and **b** above. You achieve your objective also when East holds a doubleton (or singleton) king.

Insight: Calculating the best play

In rough terms, you can calculate the best play by counting the situations in which each play will succeed. If one play will win in two situations and another in three, the second one is likely to be better. To be completely accurate, you would have to allow for the relative probabilities of the situations.

From these examples you can begin to see how to calculate the best play with an unfamiliar combination. If two possible lines come to mind, you count how many defensive holdings each one picks up. Here the first line picked up two combinations (♦K onside or diamonds 3–3). The second line also picked up further combinations (♦K-x or single ♦K offside) and was therefore a better prospect.

When you should avoid the normal play

On many hands you cannot calculate the best way to play a combination merely by looking at that particular suit in isolation.

You must consider the whole deal, in particular whether one of the defenders cannot be allowed to gain the lead. To illustrate the point, we will look at two 3NT contracts that both feature the same diamond suit. This is the first of them:

```
                    ♠ 7 6
                    ♥ K 9 6
                    ♦ A J 8 7 2
                    ♣ K 6 5
  ♠ K J 9 4 2        ┌─────────┐       ♠ Q 8 5
  ♥ Q 7 2            │    N    │       ♥ J 10 4 3
  ♦ 10 9 4          │ W     E │       ♦ Q 3
  ♣ J 4             │    S    │       ♣ Q 9 8 2
                    └─────────┘
                    ♠ A 10 3
                    ♥ A 8 5
                    ♦ K 6 5
                    ♣ A 10 7 3
```

West	North	East	South
–	–	–	1NT (15–17)
Pass	3NT	End	

West leads the ♠4 against 3NT and you hold up the ace until the third round, to break the link between the two defenders. What next?

You have seven top tricks and must establish the diamond suit in order to bump your total to nine. What is more, you cannot afford West to gain the lead or he will cash two more spade tricks, beating the contract. You will therefore play diamonds in the 'normal' way. You will cash the ♦K and then finesse the ♦J. As it happens, the finesse loses. You do not mind this at all because the safe (East) hand gains the lead and he has no spade to return. If he did have a spade left, the suit would break 4–4 and pose no threat to the contract.

Now let's switch a few cards, so that it is East who cannot be allowed to gain the lead:

```
                    ♠ 7 6
                    ♥ K 9 6
                    ♦ A J 8 7 2
                    ♣ K 6 5
    ♠ A J 9 4 2        ┌─────────┐        ♠ 10 8 5
    ♥ Q 7 2            │    N    │        ♥ J 10 4 3
    ♦ 10 9 4          │ W     E │        ♦ Q 3
    ♣ J 4             │    S    │        ♣ Q 9 8 2
                       └─────────┘
                    ♠ K Q 3
                    ♥ A 8 5
                    ♦ K 6 5
                    ♣ A 10 7 3
```

West	North	East	South
–	–	–	1NT (15–17)
Pass	3NT	End	

West leads the ♠4 against 3NT and East plays the ♠10. You win with the ♠Q and note that you have seven top tricks, as before. How should you play the diamond suit?

If you make the same play as before, cashing the ♦K and finessing the ♦J, you will go down. East, who is now the danger hand because he can lead through your ♠K-3, will gain the lead. A spade return will then sink the contract.

You do better to cash the ace and king of diamonds. As the cards lie, the ♦Q will fall doubleton and you will score an overtrick. If the ♦Q does not fall, you will lead towards the ♦J on the third round. You don't mind at all if West began with ♦Q-10-4 and wins a diamond trick. West cannot continue spades effectively from his side of the table. If he plays any other suit, you will have the four diamond tricks that you need to bring your total to nine.

(The very best play, in fact, is to lead the ♦2 from dummy. If the ♦3 or ♦4 appears from East, you can cover with the ♦5. You would then succeed when West holds ♦10-9 doubleton, also when East carelessly plays low from something like ♦Q-9-4.)

Safety plays in the trump suit

Suppose you have a trump suit of ♠A-7-6-2 opposite ♠K-J-5-4. The best play of this suit, without regard for the whole deal, is to cash the ♠A and then to finesse the ♠J. You will score all four tricks when the ♠Q is onside and the suit breaks 3–2.

In the context of a complete deal, however, this may be quite the wrong play to make. Here is a deal that illustrates the situation:

```
              ♠ A J 5 4
              ♥ 10 7
              ♦ A 9 3
              ♣ A Q J 2
 ♠ 10 8              N        ♠ Q 9 3
 ♥ K Q J 3      W       E     ♥ 9 6 5 2
 ♦ J 8 4                      ♦ 10 7 2
 ♣ 9 8 6 5          S         ♣ 10 7 4
              ♠ K 7 6 2
              ♥ A 8 4
              ♦ K Q 6 5
              ♣ K 3
```

West	North	East	South
–	–	–	1NT (15–17)
Pass	2♣	Pass	2♠
Pass	6♠	End	

West leads the ♥K against your small slam in spades and you win with the ♥A. How will you play the contract?

Suppose you had overbid to a grand slam and therefore needed to pick up the trump suit without loss. You would make the normal play in the suit, cashing the king and then finessing dummy's jack. Here, though, you can afford to lose a trump trick provided you do not also lose a heart trick. You can see what will happen if you finesse the ♠J on the first or second round. East will win with the ♠Q and the defenders will cash a heart trick to beat the slam.

A better idea is to combine the second-best play in the trump suit (playing the king and the ace) with the chance that you can discard your two heart losers on dummy's clubs. After winning the heart lead, you cash the two top trumps. The ♠Q does not fall but both defenders follow. You then turn to the club suit. All follow to the first three rounds and you discard one of your heart losers. You then lead dummy's last club winner. It makes no difference whether West decides to ruff with his master ♠Q. You will discard your last heart anyway and make the slam.

Do you see why this was a good line of play? You had less chance of avoiding a loser in the trump suit, yes, but when the first chance (two top trumps) failed, you had a substantial second chance remaining – that you could discard your heart losers. The sum of these two chances was much higher than that offered by taking a trump finesse.

Let's stick with the same trump holding and see a quite different situation where you would deviate from the normal (finessing) line of play. On this deal you are worried about the defenders scoring a ruff against you:

♠ A J 5 4
♥ 9 7 6 4
♦ K 9 3
♣ K 4

♠ 10 9 3
♥ 3
♦ 8 6 4
♣ 10 9 7 6 5 2

♠ Q 8
♥ K J 10 8 5 2
♦ 10 7 2
♣ J 8

♠ K 7 6 2
♥ A Q
♦ A Q J 5
♣ A Q 3

West	North	East	South
–	–	2♥	Dble
Pass	3♥	Pass	3♠
Pass	4♠	Pass	6♠
End			

East opens with a weak two-bid (see Chapter 5). You double for take-out and partner shows a strong hand with a cue-bid (see Chapter 10). When the spade fit comes to light, you bid a small slam. How should you play this when West leads the ♥3 to East's ♥K and your ♥A?

The bidding has told you that hearts are breaking 1–6. Suppose you play trumps in the normal way, cashing the ♠K and finessing the ♠J. There is a risk that East will win with the ♠Q and give his partner a heart ruff to defeat the slam. Not what you want! You should therefore play the ace and king of trumps, making sure that East does not gain the lead with a doubleton trump queen. As it happens, the ♠Q will fall and you will end with an overtrick. Suppose, though, that West had started with ♠Q-x-x or ♠Q-x-x-x. You would still make the contract, since you could lead towards the ♠J on the third round of the suit.

Once again, the second-best play in the trump suit, looking at it in isolation, gives you the best chance of making the contract. And that is the important thing!

POINTS TO REMEMBER

▶ *When comparing two possible ways of playing a combination in a single suit, count how many different defensive holdings can be picked up by each line of play. Choose the way that will succeed against the greatest number of holdings.*

▶ *The correct way to play a suit often varies according to how many tricks you need from it.*

▶ *Sometimes it is not good enough to look only at the suit in question. You must consider the whole deal, particularly what may happen if a particular defender gains the lead. When one defender is a 'danger hand', you must do everything you can to prevent him from gaining the lead.*

▶ *When you hold eight or nine trumps between the hands and are missing the queen, it is not always enough to apply the 'eight ever, nine never' rule as to whether you finesse or play for the drop. Sometimes you must ignore the rule, to keep a dangerous defender off lead. You may choose to ignore it also when a ruff is threatened.*

TEST YOURSELF

1

♠ A 9 6 2
♥ 2
♦ A K 7 5 3
♣ A Q 2

♦8 led

```
        N
    W       E
        S
```

♠ Q J 10 7 4
♥ A K 7
♦ Q J 2
♣ K 9

West	North	East	South
–	1♦	Pass	1♠
Pass	4♠	Pass	4NT
Pass	5♣	Pass	6♠
End			

West leads the ♦8 against your small slam in spades. How will you plan the play?

(The answer is on page 209. A second problem is overleaf.)

2

```
                    ♠ A Q 3
                    ♥ K 9 2
                    ♦ Q 7 4 2
                    ♣ K 5 2
    ♠J led    ┌──────────────┐
             │      N       │
             │   W     E    │
             │      S       │
             └──────────────┘
                    ♠ K 7 6 4
                    ♥ A 7 3
                    ♦ A 6 3
                    ♣ A 8 6
```

West	North	East	South
–	–	–	1NT (15–17)
Pass	3NT	End	

West leads the ♠J against your contract of 3NT.

a *How will you play the contract?*
b *How would you play 3NT if dummy's clubs were ♣10-5-2 instead?*

(The answer is on page 210.)

16

Destroying declarer's communications

In this chapter you will learn:
* *how to give count signals when declarer plays a suit*
* *how to hold up an ace or king to kill a suit in dummy*
* *when to hold up with two stoppers*
* *how to remove an entry to dummy.*

Holding up an ace in defence

When declarer is playing in a no-trump contract, he will often hold up the ace of the suit you have led. What is the purpose of this? To exhaust the holding of one of the defenders, so there will be no communication between the defenders' hands. Exactly the same situation can arise the other way round. A defender can hold up an ace to break the communications between declarer and the dummy.

Let's see an example of that:

```
                    ♠ 6 5 2
                    ♥ 9 6
                    ♦ 8 3 2
                    ♣ K Q 10 7 3
    ♠ 9 7            ┌──────────┐         ♠ J 10 8 4
    ♥ Q J 8 4 2      │    N     │         ♥ K 7 3
    ♦ Q 10 7 4       │ W     E  │         ♦ J 9 5
    ♣ 9 4            │    S     │         ♣ A 8 5
                     └──────────┘
                    ♠ A K Q 3
                    ♥ A 10 5
                    ♦ A K 6
                    ♣ J 6 2
```

West	North	East	South
–	–	–	2NT
Pass	3NT	End	

You are sitting East, defending 3NT, and partner leads the ♥4 to your ♥K. What does declarer do on this trick? Yes, he holds up the ace, aiming to break the communications between you and your partner. He ducks again when you return the ♥7. Declarer wins the third round of hearts and leads a club to the king. How will you defend?

Declarer has already given you a big hint with his own hold-up! You must play low, allowing dummy's ♣K to win. When declarer continues with a second round of clubs, you hold up again. You have restricted declarer to just two club tricks (rather than the four he would have scored if you had taken your ♣A too early). It will be pointless for him to play another round of clubs because he will then have no entry to dummy, to enjoy the two established cards in the suit. At this stage declarer has eight top tricks (three spades, one heart, two diamonds and two clubs). His only realistic chance of a ninth trick is that spades will break 3–3. Not today! Your hold-up of the ♣A will therefore defeat the contract.

Giving count signals

One point was glossed over in the description of that last 3NT contract. Can you think what it was? East needed to hold up his ♣A until the third round because declarer held three clubs. (If East had taken the ace on the second round, declarer would still have a club left and could cross to the dummy to score three more club tricks.) What if declarer had held only two clubs in his hand? Sitting East, you would then want to take your ♣A on the second round. If, instead, you were to duck, you would give declarer an undeserved second club trick, which might sometimes be enough for him to make the contract.

Let's change the last deal, giving South just two clubs (and making the spades 3–3):

	♠ 6 5 2	
	♥ 9 6	
	♦ 8 3 2	
	♣ K Q 10 7 3	

♠ 9 7 4		♠ J 10 8
♥ Q J 8 4 2	N	♥ K 7 3
♦ Q 4	W E	♦ J 10 9 5
♣ 9 4 2	S	♣ A 8 5

	♠ A K Q 3	
	♥ A 10 5	
	♦ A K 7 6	
	♣ J 6	

West	North	East	South
–	–	–	2NT
Pass	3NT	End	

Again declarer holds up the ♥A until the third round. As before, he then plays a club to the king, which you duck, and continues with a low club from dummy. What will happen if you hold up again, which was necessary on the previous version of the deal? Declarer will make the contract! He will have eight top tricks and the 3–3 break in spades will give him a ninth trick.

> ## Insight: When to take the ace
>
> When you are holding up an ace, to prevent declarer from enjoying a long suit in dummy, you must take your ace on the trick where declarer plays his last card in the suit. Partner will give you a count signal, so that you can determine how many cards declarer holds.

On this deal declarer holds only two clubs, so you must take your ♣A on the second round. How can you possibly know how many clubs declarer holds? There is only one way. Your partner (West) must tell you how many clubs he has. West will do this by playing high–low with an even number of clubs and low–high with an odd number of clubs. This is known as 'giving a count signal'.

When declarer holds only two clubs (♣J-6), your partner will hold ♣9-4-2. With three clubs, an odd number, he will signal with his lowest club (the ♣2) on the first round. If partner holds three clubs, declarer has only two and you should take your ♣A on the second round. The only other possibility is that partner holds a singleton club and declarer has four cards in the suit. Then it will not matter when you take your ace. So, on the version of the deal where declarer held two clubs, you would take your ace on the second round and beat the contract.

Now look back a couple of pages to the original version of the deal, where declarer held three clubs. Your partner would then play the ♣9 on the first round, his higher card, to show a doubleton. Placing declarer with three clubs (or four if partner has a singleton), you would hold up your ♣A until the third round and again beat the contract.

Great, isn't it? By playing count signals when declarer leads a suit like this, you will know how to defend all the time!

Most bridge players use attitude signals (high to encourage, low to discourage) when partner leads a suit. They use count signals (high to show an even number of cards, low to show an odd number) when declarer leads a suit.

Insight: Counting distribution

The more you play bridge, the more you will realize how important it is to gain a count on each suit. In other words, you try to discover how many cards each player holds in the suit. When you have such information, the game becomes much easier – both when defending and when playing the dummy.

Holding up a king in defence

Even when you hold the king of dummy's long suit, rather than the ace, you may be able to kill declarer's communications. Let's see an example of that:

```
                    ♠ 7 6 2
                    ♥ 9 6
                    ♦ A Q J 8 4 2
                    ♣ J 7
   ♠ Q J 10 9 5        N            ♠ 8 4
   ♥ J 7          W         E       ♥ K Q 4 3 2
   ♦ 9 3                            ♦ K 10 6
   ♣ 10 8 4 3          S            ♣ Q 9 5
                    ♠ A K 3
                    ♥ A 10 8 5
                    ♦ 7 5
                    ♣ A K 6 2
```

West	North	East	South
–	–	–	1♣
Pass	1♦	Pass	2NT
Pass	3NT	End	

You are sitting East and your partner leads the ♠Q against 3NT. Declarer wins with the ♠K and leads the ♦5 to West's ♦9 and dummy's ♦Q. How will you defend?

Suppose you win with the ♦K, returning a spade. Declarer will win with the ♠A and make an overtrick. He still has an entry to dummy, so he will score five diamond tricks. What could you have done about it?

West's ♦9 is a count signal and suggests that he may hold two diamonds, leaving declarer with two cards in the suit. You should hold up your ♦K, allowing dummy's ♦Q to win. Declarer cannot now score more than two diamond tricks and will go down in his contract. Indeed, if you duck smoothly declarer may return to his hand with the ♣A to repeat the diamond finesse. This time it will lose and he will then make only one diamond trick!

When the suit length is in declarer's hand, hidden from view, it can be more difficult to hold up a king. Take the East cards on this deal:

```
              ♠ 8 2
              ♥ A 8 4 3
              ♦ A K Q 7
              ♣ A Q 2
♠ K J 9 7 6   ┌─────────┐   ♠ Q 5 4
♥ K 10 7 2    │    N    │   ♥ Q 9 6
♦ 10 2        │ W     E │   ♦ J 9 8 5
♣ 10 7        │    S    │   ♣ K 9 6
              └─────────┘
              ♠ A 10 3
              ♥ J 5
              ♦ 6 4 3
              ♣ J 8 5 4 3
```

West	North	East	South
–	1♦	Pass	1NT
Pass	3NT	End	

West leads the ♣7 against 3NT and your queen wins the first trick. You persist with the ♣5, partner winning South's ♣10 with the ♣J.

West then clears the spade suit, declarer winning with the ace. At Trick 4 declarer leads the ♣3, covered by West's 10 and dummy's queen. What is your plan for the defence?

Your first task is to read the lie of the club suit. Partner has played the ♣10. What does that mean? It indicates that he has either a doubleton ♣10-x or a singleton. He cannot hold ♣J-10 doubleton, or he would have played the jack. So, declarer is marked with five (or six) clubs to the jack. You must not release your king of clubs!

Suppose you are playing on auto-pilot and capture dummy's ♣Q with the king. Declarer will win your return and score four club tricks and three diamond tricks, to go with the major-suit aces. Instead, you should allow dummy's ♣Q to win. Declarer will no doubt continue with ♣A, hoping that the ♣K will fall. No such luck on this occasion and he will go two down. If he establishes the club suit, by playing a third round, he will have no way to reach the long cards in his own hand.

Holding up in defence with two stoppers

When dummy has one side entry, it may work well to hold up when you have two stoppers in dummy's long suit. Take the East cards on this deal:

West	North	East	South
–	–	–	1♣
Pass	1♦	Pass	2NT
Pass	3NT	End	

West leads the ♥2 against 3NT and your ♥J is won by South's ♥K. Declarer continues with a diamond to dummy's jack, West signalling count with the ♦2. How will you defend?

It may seem natural to win with the ♦Q. Suppose you do this, returning the ♥6. Declarer will win with the ♥A and lead his last diamond to dummy, establishing the suit. It will do you no good to hold up the ♦A now, because the ♠K will be an entry to dummy. The defenders will score two hearts and two diamonds, but declarer will claim the remaining tricks. He will score three diamond tricks to go with his three ace-king combinations.

To kill dummy's diamond suit, you must duck on the first round, allowing the ♦J to win. When you capture the second round of diamonds, declarer will have no card left in the suit. If he uses the ♠K to reach dummy and set up the diamond suit, he cannot return to dummy to enjoy the established cards in the suit.

You would make exactly the same play if dummy held ♦Q-J-10-9-x and you held ♦A-K-x in defence. You would hold up on the first round so that declarer had no diamond remaining when you captured the second round.

Suppose instead that this was the lie of the diamond suit:

```
              North
              ♦ Q J 10 9 5
    West                      East
    ♦ A 8 2                   ♦ K 6 3
              South
              ♦ 7 4
```

The diamond stoppers are divided between the two defenders' hands. The principle is exactly the same, however. When dummy contains a side entry in a different suit, neither defender must win the first round of diamonds. If East wins the first round with the ♦K, for example, declarer will have a diamond left in his hand and will be able to clear the suit.

Removing an entry to dummy

When dummy holds a long suit accompanied by one side-suit entry, the defenders' top priority may be to remove this entry. Suppose you had been East on the following deal. Would you have defended correctly?

```
              ♠ A
              ♥ 9 8 3
              ♦ K Q J 10 7 5
              ♣ 8 6 2
♠ 10 7 6 4        N        ♠ J 8 5 2
♥ Q 10 7 2    W       E    ♥ A 6 4
♦ 8 2             S        ♦ A 6 3
♣ Q 10 7                   ♣ J 9 3
              ♠ K Q 9 3
              ♥ K J 5
              ♦ 9 4
              ♣ A K 5 4
```

West	North	East	South
–	–	–	1♣
Pass	1♦	Pass	1NT
Pass	3NT	End	

Your partner, West, leads the ♥2 and you win with the ♥A. What should you do next?

There are two possible guidelines to follow at this stage. One is 'always return your partner's suit'; another is the recommendation posted on the office walls of one of the world's top computer companies: 'THINK!'

Suppose you do return a heart. Declarer, who knows from the ♥2 lead that hearts are breaking 4–3, will rise with the ♥K. He will then establish the diamond suit. It will do you no good to hold up the ♦A for a round or two because the ♠A is still available as an entry. The defenders will take three heart tricks and one diamond. Declarer will then score the remaining tricks to make his contract.

Insight: Defensive guidelines

When you start to play, teachers will give you basic guidelines for defence such as 'second hand plays low', 'cover an honour with an honour' and 'return partner's suit'. These can only take you so far. There are many exceptions to all these rules, as you will quickly realize. Good defending is a matter of hard work and thinking clearly. Sorry if that is bad news!

Instead of returning partner's suit, you should play a spade to remove the ♠A entry to dummy. You can then hold up the ♦A for one round (West would have led a spade from a five-card suit, so South's likely shape is 4–3–2–4). You win the second round of diamonds and continue hearts, West winning and clearing the suit. Declarer will have only seven top tricks. He can establish an eighth trick, in the club suit, but that will still be one down.

POINTS TO REMEMBER

▶ *When you hold the ace of a long suit in the dummy, you should generally hold up until the round that will exhaust declarer's holding in the suit (the second round, for example, if declarer holds two cards). Partner will give you a count signal, allowing you to determine how many cards declarer has in the suit.*

▶ *Similarly, you may be able to kill a long suit in dummy (or sometimes in declarer's hand) by holding up a king.*

▶ *Even when you hold two stoppers in dummy's suit, it can be right to hold up on the first round. This is the case when declarer holds a doubleton and dummy has one side-entry in a different suit.*

▶ *When dummy contains a threatening side suit that will soon be established, see if you can kill the suit by removing a potential entry card.*

TEST YOURSELF

1

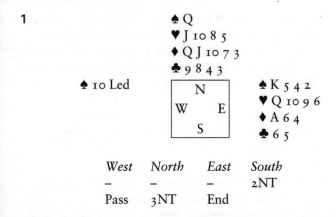

	♠ Q
	♥ J 10 8 5
	♦ Q J 10 7 3
	♣ 9 8 4 3

♠ 10 Led

```
        N
    W       E
        S
```

♠ K 5 4 2
♥ Q 10 9 6
♦ A 6 4
♣ 6 5

West	North	East	South
–	–	–	2NT
Pass	3NT	End	

You are sitting East and West leads the ♠10, covered by the queen, king and South's ace. Declarer continues with the ♦K and (if this is allowed to win) the ♦2. How will you defend if West follows with the ♦5 and the ♦8? How would you defend if West follows instead with the ♦8 and then the ♦5?

(The answer is on page 211.)

2

♠ A 6 2
♥ J 6
♦ Q J 10 8 6 3
♣ 8 5

♥ K Led

♠ 9 8 3
♥ 5 2
♦ A K 4
♣ J 10 6 4 3

West	North	East	South
–	–	–	1♣
Pass	1♦	Pass	2NT
Pass	3NT	End	

West, your partner, leads the ♥K against 3NT. Declarer ducks the first trick and West continues with the ♥Q, which is also allowed to win. When West plays the ♥10, dummy discards a club and you throw a low spade. Declarer wins with the ♥A and leads the ♦9, West following with the ♦7. What is your plan for the defence?

(The answer is on page 212.)

17

Two-suited overcalls

In this chapter you will learn:
- *the Unusual No-trump overcall*
- *the Unusual No-trump over a minor suit*
- *how to respond to the Unusual No-trump*
- *Michaels cue-bids*
- *how to respond to a Michaels cue-bid*
- *the 2NT response to Michaels.*

The Unusual No-trump

Suppose your right-hand opponent opens 1♠ and you overcall 2NT. What should such a bid mean? Without any discussion, you might assume that it showed a balanced hand with good spade stopper – a hand that was a few points stronger than a 1NT overcall, perhaps around 19–21 points. That's fair enough, but many years ago players realized that you could launch a strong balanced hand with a take-out double, rebidding some number of no-trumps later. They invented a new meaning for a jump overcall of 2NT. It would show at least five cards in both of the minor suits. This convention is standard in tournament bridge and widely used in rubber bridge too. It is known as the Unusual No-trump, usually abbreviated to UNT.

Suppose you are second to speak and the player in front of you has opened 1♠ (or 1♥). You have to find a bid on one of these hands:

a ♠ 6   b ♠ J 2   c ♠ 6
   ♥ 9 4   ♥ 3   ♥ 2
   ♦ A Q J 8 7   ♦ K 9 7 6 2   ♦ K Q J 10 2
   ♣ K J 10 5 2   ♣ Q 10 8 5 3   ♣ A K J 10 7 2

Hand **a** is perfect for the UNT. Both your suits are well-packed with honours and you would be very unlucky to go for a big penalty at the three-level. Hand **b** is not so suitable and most players would not venture 2NT, even when non-vulnerable against vulnerable. Hand **c** is super-strong. You would start with 2NT and bid again over partner's response, to let him know that you held an unusually strong hand and there might be a chance of game. (Over a 3♦ response, you would rebid 4♣ to tell him that your clubs were longer.)

Insight: Mis-use of conventions

When bridge players have a bidding gadget available, they are often tempted to use it even when their hand is unsuitable. The Unusual No-trump is a convention that is frequently mis-used. To avoid suffering a large penalty, your suits must have some quality to them, particularly when you are vulnerable.

When you bid 2NT you are naturally hoping that your side may end up playing the contract with one of the minor suits as trumps. However, another important objective is that you are taking a lot of bidding space away from the opponents. The player to your left, for example, will no longer be able to respond 2♥ to 1♠, or to raise 1♠ to 2♠. So, 2NT can be useful in two ways. It can help you bid constructively on a hand with the minor suits (you could not double on such a hand because of your shortage in the other major). You can also interfere seriously with the opponents' bidding.

Unusual No-trump over a minor suit

When the opponents have opened with a one-bid in a minor suit, you can use 2NT to show the lowest two unbid suits. So, over 1♣ a 2NT overcall would show hearts and diamonds. Over 1♦, it would show heart and clubs.

Responding to the Unusual No-trump

How do you respond when partner overcalls 2NT? Most of the time, you will simply bid three of your better minor. Remember that an 11-trick game in a minor suit requires considerable values. When you have a particularly good fit, you can bid one of the minors at the four-level or the five-level.

Particularly when non-vulnerable, you may jump to 5♣ or 5♦ on a hand with a big trump fit but limited general values. Your intention will be to make life difficult for the opponents, who will doubtless hold a great fit in one of the major suits. Bear the vulnerability in mind at all times. When partner is vulnerable, he will have a reasonable hand to venture a 2NT overcall.

Suppose the opponents only are vulnerable and the bidding starts like this:

West	North	East	South
1♥	2NT	Pass	?

What would you respond on the following South hands?

a	♠ Q 8 3 2	b	♠ K 9 4	c	♠ A 10 6 5 4
	♥ A Q 6 4		♥ Q 10 8 6 5 2		♥ 2
	♦ Q 8 7		♦ 8 7		♦ K J 9 7 2
	♣ 9 5		♣ 10 2		♣ K 3

On hand **a** you respond at the minimum level, bidding 3♦. It is unlikely that you can make a game and you must choose the response that will be right most of the time. With **b** you were not at all happy to hear partner's UNT. Don't make this obvious to the world by frowning (or, heaven forbid, muttering 'That's very awkward')! Bid 3♣ straight away and let the opponents worry what to do. Hand **c** represents a fantastic fit for partner. You should go all the way to 5♦. If the opponents double, thinking that you have bid high in an effort to shut them out, they may end up being disappointed when your partner makes the contract.

Bidding 2NT after two passes

Until now we have been discussing a 2NT overcall by the player sitting over the opening bidder. What should 2NT mean in an auction like this?

West	North	East	South
1♥	Pass	Pass	2NT

Some players give 2NT the same meaning as in the second seat; it is the Unusual No-trump. The majority of players prefer the bid to be natural, though, showing around 18–20 points, perhaps bolstered by one long minor suit. So, if you start playing the Unusual No-trump you must discuss with your partner whether it applies also in the fourth seat, after two passes.

The Michaels cue-bid

You will realize by now that tournament players do not like to leave any bid without a meaning! Suppose your right-hand opponent opens 1♣. What do you think an overcall of 2♣ should mean?

Many decades ago, an overcall in the opponents' suit showed a very strong hand of some sort. This was a complete waste of the bid, since you can launch such hands with a take-out double, bidding strongly thereafter. So, tournament players prefer to use a cue-bid in the opponents' suit to show a two-suited hand of at least 5–5 shape. This is the scheme:

> 2♣ over 1♣   shows both major suits
> 2♦ over 1♦   shows both major suits
> 2♥ over 1♥   shows spades and one of the minors
> 2♠ over 1♠   shows hearts and one of the minors

Known as the Michaels cue-bid, the bid shows as many major suits as is possible – both of them over a minor-suit opening, the other major over a major-suit opening. The point-count of the hand may be quite modest, about the same as for a one-level overcall. That's because there is more chance of outbidding the opponents when you hold the major suits. Suppose your right-hand opponent has opened 1♣ and you have to find a bid on one of these hands:

	a		b		c
♠	K J 8 4 2	♠	A Q 10 9 5	♠	J 9 7 6 2
♥	K 10 9 6 4	♥	K Q J 8 2	♥	10 8 6 4 3
♦	7	♦	A 2	♦	K J
♣	9 5	♣	8	♣	A

Hand **a** is fine for a non-vulnerable 2♣ overcall. When vulnerable, many players would pass, since their partner would expect a slightly stronger hand. Hand **b** is considerably stronger. You would begin with 2♣ and then raise partner's 2♥ or 2♠ response to the three-level to invite game. Hand **c** is not particularly suitable, because 8 of the 9 points lie in the short suits. Nevertheless, some players would venture a non-vulnerable Michaels cue-bid. At least they would interrupt the opponents' auction.

When you make a major-suit Michaels bid, particularly 2♠ over 1♠, the bidding is likely to be carried higher than after a minor-suit Michaels bid. Your hand should be correspondingly stronger, to avoid conceding a sizable penalty at the three-level. Suppose your right-hand opponent has opened 1♠ and you hold one of these hands:

a	♠ 4 2	b	♠ 5	c	♠ 2
	♥ A 9 8 6 4		♥ K Q J 8 2		♥ K Q 10 8 7 2
	♦ A Q 7 4 2		♦ 7 2		♦ A J 8 7 2
	♣ 10		♣ A Q 10 8 2		♣ 5

Hand **a** contains two moderate suits and you might go for a large penalty at the three-level if you found partner with an unsuitable hand. Some players might risk a 2♠ Michaels bid when non-vulnerable, but this would not be a sound bid. It would simply be a gamble that you would find partner with some sort of fit and disrupt the enemy auction. It is best to pass on such a hand.

Hand **b** is more like it! You hold two good suits and a perfect hand for a 2♠ overcall. On hand **c**, with a good six-card heart suit, you should overcall 2♥. If partner has two hearts and three diamonds, you don't really want to play in diamonds rather than hearts. Apart from that, you are more likely to reach a playable 4♥ if you emphasize your good hearts.

Responding to a Michaels cue-bid

When partner has made a Michaels cue-bid, you should assume that he has a minimum for his bid and respond accordingly. It is similar to responding to a take-out double. If you have a good fit, or a strong hand, you can show your strength by jumping. Suppose the bidding starts like this:

West	North	East	South
1♦	2♦	Pass	?

... and you have to find a response on one of these South hands:

a	♠ 9 7	b	♠ K 10 8 7 2	c	♠ 9 2
	♥ Q 10		♥ Q 4		♥ 8
	♦ A 7 2		♦ A 9 8 2		♦ J 10 7 2
	♣ K J 9 6 4		♣ 10 7		♣ A Q 9 8 6 3

On hand **a** you should respond just 2♥. Remember that partner may hold a modest hand of around 8 points or so. If he has a singleton club, for example, he will not find your club holding very useful. Hand **b** represents a fantastic fit for spades and you should leap all the way to 4♠. Even opposite a minimum Michaels overcall you expect to have a reasonable play for game. On hand **c** you bid 2♠, responding at the minimum level in your better major. It's not your fault that you don't have three-card support for one of partner's suits.

When partner has made a major-suit Michaels bid and you want to play in his minor suit, you respond 3♣:

West	East	West	North	East	South
♠ Q 3	♠ J 9 7 4	–	–	–	1♠
♥ A Q 10 5 4	♥ K 3	2♠	Pass	3♣	Pass
♦ K J 10 6 2	♦ Q 9 8 3	3♦	End		
♣ 3	♣ J 10 5				

West's 2♠ overcall shows at least 5–5 shape in hearts and an unspecified minor. East sees that he will have a fit in partner's minor suit, whichever one it is. He responds 3♣, which West will pass if his minor suit is clubs. Here West's second suit is diamonds, so he corrects to 3♦, which becomes the final contract.

....
Insight: Pass or correct
East's 3♣ bid on this auction is described as a 'pass or correct' bid. Such bids are used when partner has used a convention that has not yet specified which suits he holds. (There are several such conventions in tournament bridge.) West will pass if his second suit is clubs and correct to 3♦ with diamonds.
....

The 2NT response to Michaels 2♥/2♠

Just occasionally you will hold a very strong hand in response to a Michaels overcall in a major suit. In that situation you may wish to find out more about partner's hand in order to bid the best contract. You respond 2NT, which asks partner to describe his hand further. Suppose the bidding starts:

West	North	East	South
1♥	2♥	Pass	2NT
Pass	?		

South has asked partner to describe his hand further. North rebids according to this schedule:

3♣	Lower	=	range hand with spades and clubs
3♦	Lower	=	range hand with spades and diamonds
3♥	Upper	=	range hand with spades and clubs
3♠	Upper	=	range hand with spades and diamonds

A lower-range hand would be around 8–13 points. Upper-range would be 14+ points. On some hands, the responder might pass a rebid of 3♣ or 3♦. Facing an upper-range rebid, he would probably bid game in one of the overcaller's suits.

POINTS TO REMEMBER

▶ *In the second seat (sitting to the left of the opening bidder), you can bid 2NT to show a hand that is at least 5–5 in the minor suits. This convention is known as the Unusual No-trump.*

▶ *Most players use 2NT in the fourth seat (after a start such as 1♥ – Pass – Pass) to show a strong balanced hand. If you want to treat 2NT as the Unusual No-trump in the fourth seat, you should agree this with your partner.*

▶ *In both the second and fourth seats, a cue-bid in the enemy suit (such as 2♣ over 1♣) is a Michaels cue-bid. A cue-bid in a minor suit shows both the major suits. A cue-bid in a major suit shows the other major and an unspecified minor. The overall strength may be moderate, particularly when non-vulnerable.*

▶ *After a major-suit Michaels cue-bid (such as 1♥ – 2♥), responder may bid 3♣ to say that he wants to play in three of partner's minor suit.*

▶ *After a major-suit Michaels cue-bid, responder may bid 2NT to ask for more information about the overcaller's hand. With a lower-range overcall, partner rebids 3♣ or 3♦ to show his minor. With an upper-range hand, he will rebid 3♥ (with clubs) or 3♠ (with diamonds).*

TEST YOURSELF

1 *The bidding starts like this:*

West	North	East	South
1♥	?		

What would you say on the following North hands?

a
♠ –
♥ 10 2
♦ Q J 10 8 3 2
♣ K Q J 9 4

b
♠ A Q 8
♥ A J 10 6
♦ K 9 4
♣ A Q 3

c
♠ A Q 10 7 6
♥ 7
♦ 8 2
♣ A 10 9 7 4

2 *What will you respond on the following South hands when, at Love All, your partner makes an UNT overcall?*

West	North	East	South
1♠	2NT	Pass	?

a
♠ A 10 8 6 5 2
♥ 8 2
♦ Q 10 8
♣ 4 2

b
♠ K Q 9 6 4
♥ Q 10 8 7 3
♦ 6
♣ J 7

c
♠ A 9 8 5 2
♥ 9
♦ 7 2
♣ A Q J 8 2

3 *What will you respond on the following South hands when, at Love All, your partner makes a Michaels cue-bid?*

West	North	East	South
1♥	2♥	Pass	?

a
♠ A 10 8 6
♥ A 8
♦ K 10 7 3
♣ K 9 4

b
♠ 4
♥ Q 10 8 7 3
♦ J 10 7 6
♣ A 8 3

c
♠ A 9 2
♥ 9
♦ A Q 8 6 3
♣ A 10 8 4

(The answers are on page 213.)

18

Counting the hand

In this chapter you will learn:
- *how to count the defenders' hands*
- *how to use the information gained*.

One of the most important techniques in bridge is an apparently simple one – counting. It may seem easy but it takes discipline to force yourself to do it, hand after hand. What should you count? As declarer you need to count the shape of the defenders' hands. Once you know how many cards a defender holds in each suit, the play will become very much easier. You can also count high-card points. If someone opened a 15–17 point 1NT and has already shown up with 16 points outside clubs, you will know that he cannot hold the ♣Q. Finally, you can count tricks. Particularly in defence, it is important to count the tricks that you need to beat the contract. Suppose you are defending 3NT, for example, and can see three certain tricks. You must look for two more from some quarter.

In this chapter we will look at counting shape and the benefits that can flow from the knowledge that you gain.

Counting to assist a two-way guess

When a contract depends on a two-way guess for a queen, don't rush to take this decision. Play on the other suits and try to determine which defender holds more cards in the key suit. The player with the greater number of cards will be favourite to hold the missing queen. Deals such as the following are commonplace:

```
                    ♠ 9 4 2
                    ♥ A 9 5
                    ♦ A K 5
                    ♣ K J 6 3
    ♠ A K J 10 6        N          ♠ 8 3
    ♥ 8 6                          ♥ 10 4 2
    ♦ J 9          W       E       ♦ Q 10 7 6 4 2
    ♣ Q 9 7 4           S          ♣ 8 2
                    ♠ Q 7 5
                    ♥ K Q J 7 3
                    ♦ 8 3
                    ♣ A 10 5
```

West	North	East	South
–	–	–	1♥
1♠	2♣	Pass	3♥
Pass	4♥	End	

North's 2♣ shows a sound heart raise and game in hearts is duly reached. West leads the ♠A and receives an encouraging ♠8 from his partner. He continues with king and another spade, East ruffing the third round. East switches to a trump and you draw trumps in two more rounds. How will you continue?

You have lost three tricks already and the contract depends on you guessing which defender holds the ♣Q. If you think East holds the missing queen, you will finesse the ♣10. If, instead, you think West holds the card, you will finesse the ♣J. Which defender is more likely to hold the ♣Q, do you think?

The bidding provides little clue, because West has already shown enough strength to merit a one-level overcall. The defender who holds more clubs than his partner will be favourite to hold the queen of the suit. At the moment West has shown up with seven cards in the majors and East began with only five. So, East is currently the favourite to hold the ♣Q.

Instead of playing on clubs immediately, you cash the ace and king of diamonds and ruff a diamond. West shows out on the third round and you now have a 'complete count of the hand'. West started with a 5–2–2–4 shape. He has four clubs to East's two and is therefore twice as likely as East to hold the ♣Q. You cash the ♣A and finesse dummy's ♣J. On this occasion justice is done. West does indeed hold the missing ♣Q and you make the contract.

Insight: Counting a suit

Here are some techniques to help you count a suit. Suppose you hold ♦A 8 2 opposite ♦K 7 6 in no-trumps. You duck the first round and then cash the ace and king, so you can see three rounds of the suit. In a suit contract, perhaps you hold ♠A K 9 4 opposite ♠5. By cashing the ace and king and ruffing twice in your hand, you can get a complete count on the defenders' spades.

Sometimes you can be certain that a finesse will work:

	♠ A Q 2	
	♥ A J 5	
	♦ A K 9 3	
	♣ K J 3	
♠ J 10 5 3		♠ 7 6 4
♥ 9 8 6		♥ 10 7 4 2
♦ 2		♦ J 8 6 4
♣ 10 9 8 6 4		♣ 7 2
	♠ K 9 8	
	♥ K Q 3	
	♦ Q 10 7 5	
	♣ A Q 5	

West	North	East	South
–	–	–	1NT (15–17)
Pass	7NT	End	

West leads the ♣10 against 7NT. How will you play the contract?

You have 12 tricks on top and can make a thirteenth trick from the diamonds, provided the suit breaks 3–2 or you guess correctly which defender holds ♦J-x-x-x. (If it is East, you will need to cash the ace and king first; if it is West, you will need to cash the ace and queen.) You should aim to get an accurate count on the spades, hearts and clubs before guessing which honours to cash first in the diamond suit.

You win the club lead and cash two more rounds of clubs. East shows out on the third round, so you have a count on that suit. When you continue with three rounds of spades and three rounds of hearts, both defenders follow all the way. West has shown up with at least 11 cards in spades, hearts and clubs. He cannot possibly hold four diamonds! So, you cash the ace and king of diamonds, knowing for sure that this is the right thing to do. West shows out on the second round of diamonds, and you finesse the ♦10, making the grand slam.

Insight: Counting the hand

Counting the hand is a gradual process. The opening lead may give you a count on the suit led; for example, the lead of the ♥2 will suggest that the leader holds four hearts. When you draw trumps, this will give you a count on two suits. Get a count on just one more suit and your count will be complete.

Suppose, instead, that West had shown out on the third round of both spades and hearts. His shape would then be 2–2–4–5 and you would play the diamond suit differently, cashing the ace of diamonds and then the queen. A finesse of dummy's ♦9 would then land the grand slam.

When an opponent has made a pre-emptive bid it is often quite easy to obtain a count on the hand. Would you have kept track of the suit lengths on the next deal?

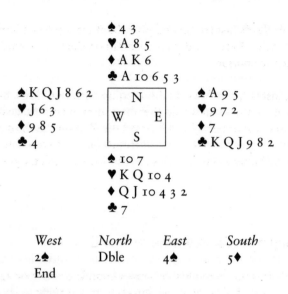

♠ 4 3
♥ A 8 5
♦ A K 6
♣ A 10 6 5 3

♠ K Q J 8 6 2   ♠ A 9 5
♥ J 6 3   ♥ 9 7 2
♦ 9 8 5   ♦ 7
♣ 4   ♣ K Q J 9 8 2

♠ 10 7
♥ K Q 10 4
♦ Q J 10 4 3 2
♣ 7

West	North	East	South
2♠	Dble	4♠	5♦
End			

West opens with a weak two-bid, showing six spades and around
6–10 points. North doubles for take-out and East raises pre-
emptively to 4♠. Your bid of 5♦ ends the auction and the defenders
cash two rounds of spades, West then switching to a trump. How
will you play the contract?

The only problem is a potential loser on the fourth round of hearts.
If clubs break 4–3, you can set up a long club for a heart discard
and avoid the need to take any guess on the third round of hearts.
You win the trump switch with the ♦10, cross to the ♣A and ruff
a club with the ♦Q. Unfortunately, West shows out on this trick.
What now?

Since there is no future in setting up the clubs, you might as well
draw trumps. You play a trump to dummy's ace and East shows
out. Have you been keeping a count of the hand? West started with
six spades, shown in the bidding, and has since shown up with one
club and three diamonds. So, his shape is 6–3–3–1 and the hearts
are breaking evenly!

You draw West's last trump and play the three top heart honours. As if by magic, West's ♥J does indeed fall on the third round and you make the contract.

Suppose, instead, that West had turned up with two clubs, making his shape 6–2–3–2. You would then have drawn trumps, cashed the king and ace of hearts and finessed the ♥10 on the third round of the suit. You can see how useful it is to obtain a complete count on the deal. Many a time it will save you from a difficult guess in a side suit.

Obtaining a partial count on the hand

Sometimes it is not possible to obtain a complete count on the hand. Even a partial count may allow you to swing the odds in your favour. Look at this deal:

```
                ♠ K 9 7
                ♥ K 6 4
                ♦ K 10 8
                ♣ K Q 8 3
  ♠ 10 5          N          ♠ Q J 6 3 2
  ♥ 10 8 7                   ♥ J 9 5 3
  ♦ Q 7 5 4 2   W   E        ♦ 9 6
  ♣ 9 6 4          S         ♣ 10 2
                ♠ A 8 4
                ♥ A Q 2
                ♦ A J 3
                ♣ A J 7 5
```

West	North	East	South
–	–	–	2NT
Pass	6NT	End	

How would you play 6NT when West leads the ♣6? You have 11 top tricks and will need to guess which defender holds the ♦Q, in order to score a third diamond trick and bring your total to 12.

You win the club lead and play two more rounds of clubs, getting a count on that suit. Let's say that East throws a spade. Your next move is to duck a round of spades. Do you see the point of this? By ducking the first round and later cashing the ace and king, you will be able to see three rounds of spades safely. Let's say that the defenders win the ducked spade and return a heart.

You play all your winners outside the diamond suit and sit back to digest the information that you have obtained. West began with two spades and three clubs. He began with at most four hearts and perhaps only three (you do not know who holds the last heart at this stage). West therefore began with four or five of the seven missing diamonds, which makes him the favourite to hold the ♦Q. You cash the ♦A, therefore, and finesse dummy's ♦10. Justice is done on this occasion and the slam is yours.

As you see, it is possible to bend the odds in your favour by counting, even when you cannot obtain a complete count on the hand.

POINTS TO REMEMBER

▶ *When you have a two-way queen guess, play on the other suits first and aim to get a 'complete count on the hand'. The defender who started with more cards in the key suit is more likely to hold the missing queen.*

▶ *You can often use detective work to discover how a suit lies. For example, with ♦A K 8 2 in dummy and ♦5 in your hand, you can ruff two rounds to see whether the defenders follow suit.*

▶ *Many hands become easier to play if you keep track of how many cards each defender holds in each suit.*

▶ *Even when you cannot get a complete count on the hand, a partial count may tell you that East has at least four of the seven missing spades. He will then become the favourite to hold the missing ♠Q.*

1

♠ Q 5
♥ Q 9 6 2
♦ A Q 4
♣ A 7 4 2

♠K led

N
W   E
S

♠ 4
♥ A K J 10 3
♦ K J 5
♣ K Q 9 6

West	North	East	South
3♠	Pass	Pass	4♥
Pass	5♥	Pass	6♥
End			

How will you play the small slam when West leads the ♠K – East signalling count with the ♠2 – and continues with the ♠A?

(The answer is on page 214.)

2

<pre>
                        ♠ Q 9 5
                        ♥ Q J 6 2
                        ♦ Q J 4
                        ♣ A 10 4
♥10 led   ┌───────────┐
                  │   N   │
                  │ W   E │
                  │   S   │
                  └───────────┘
                        ♠ A K 3
                        ♥ A K 4
                        ♦ K 8 5 3
                        ♣ K J 6
</pre>

West	North	East	South
–	–	–	2NT
Pass	4NT	Pass	6NT
End			

West leads the ♥10 and you win with the ♥A. How will you play the small slam?

(The answer is on page 215.)

19

Duplicate bridge

In this chapter you will learn:
- *how duplicate bridge is played*
- *how to use bidding boxes*
- *how to alert a conventional bid*
- *how a duplicate pairs event is scored.*

What is duplicate bridge?

Perhaps you have never played duplicate bridge, in a club, and are wondering whether to undertake such an adventure. In this final chapter of the book, we will look at the differences between a home game of rubber bridge and a duplicate pairs session.

First of all, what does the term 'duplicate bridge' mean? It means that every hand will be played more than once, in an attempt to reduce the luck factor. Your own score on each deal will be compared with other pairs who have played exactly the same cards as you. If you score better than they do, you will have a 'good board'; if they score better, you will have a 'poor board'. We will look at the scoring method in a moment. What actually happens when you and your partner arrive at the club?

You will be assigned a 'pair number' and an initial 'seating position'. For example, the organizer may tell you that you are

Pair 11 and will start as North–South at Table 3. You go to those positions and play begins. On the first round of the event, you will probably have to deal the cards for each board. You bid and play the hand, as at rubber bridge, but instead of gathering the four cards at the end of each trick, you play all 13 of your cards in a line in front of you. If you win a trick, you place the card lengthways, pointing at your partner. If the other side wins a trick, you place it sideways, pointing towards your opponents. So at any stage, you can easily see how many tricks you have won and lost.

When the deal is completed, each player returns his 13 cards to a plastic or wooden container, known as a board. This contains four slots marked 'North', 'East', 'South' and 'West'. In this way the deal is preserved and other contestants can play it later. The board also contains a 'travelling score-sheet', on which the contract and result will be marked. The entry for the board you have just played may, for example, look like:

N–S pair	E–W pair	Contract	Played by	N–S	E–W
11	4	4♠ + 1	S	650	

This would indicate that, as North–South, Pair 11 made one overtrick in Four Spades and scored +650. When you are vulnerable (this will be marked on the board itself) the game bonus is 500. So the score of 650 is made up of five major-suit tricks at 30 points each, plus the vulnerable game bonus. A non-vulnerable game bonus is 300 and a part-score bonus is worth 50. The first time you play, the other contestants will assist you with the scoring. North is the player responsible for filling in the score-sheet.

A typical 'round', played against the same opponents, will consist of two, three or four boards. The organizer will then call 'Move, please!' and you may then have to move to another table. A 'movement card' on the table will tell you where your next move is. It may say, for example, 'Go to East–West, Table 6'.

Bidding boxes

In most clubs you will make your bids and calls via the cards in a 'bidding box', rather than by word of mouth. If you want to bid 2♦, you put your thumb on the 2♦ bidding card and lift it, together with all the cards behind it (which represent the bids lower than 2♦), placing it on the table in front of you. Should you make another bid, Pass, Double or Redouble later, you will place the bidding card or cards on top of the 2♦ card, offset to the right. In this way the calls displayed in front of you will represent all the calls that you have made. Your line might, for example, be:

2♦   3NT   Pass

Your partner, who we will say, opened the bidding with 1♠, might have a line of calls like this:

1♠   2♠   4♠

If the opponents passed throughout, they will each have a line of green Pass cards before them. So, everyone can see that the bidding was:

West	North	East	South
–	1♠	Pass	2♦
Pass	2♠	Pass	3NT
Pass	4♠	End	

Calling the director

If any potential infraction of the Laws arises, the players should call the director. He or she will then come to the table and make a 'ruling', possibly after referring to the relevant section of the Rule Book. For example, the director should be called if a revoke occurs.

Alerting conventional bids

When your partner makes a bid that is conventional in your agreed system, you should say 'Alert!' or wave the blue Alert card from the bidding box. The opponents then have the right to ask what the bid meant. For example, if an opponent opens 1♦ and your partner overcalls with a Michaels cue-bid of 2♦, you should wave the alert card.

How is the scoring done?

In a duplicate pairs event, the scoring is done at the end of the session. Your score on each board will be compared with that of each other pair in your direction who played the board. You will score two matchpoints for each pair that you managed to beat and one matchpoint for each pair with whom you tied. Suppose four other pairs played the board, you beat two of them and tied with another. You would score 2 + 2 + 1 = 5 matchpoints out of a possible 'top' of eight matchpoints.

A score-sheet for a board in a five-table event might look like this:

			Score		Matchpoints	
N-S pair	E-W pair	Contract	N-S	E-W	N-S	E-W
1	6	4♥ + 1	650		5	3
2	9	4♥ + 2	680		8	0
3	7	6♥ − 1		100	2	6
4	8	4♥ + 1	650		5	3
5	10	6♥ x − 1		200	0	8

Pair 2 obtained a 'complete top' in the North–South direction, scoring eight matchpoints for making two overtricks in Four Hearts. Pair 5 obtained a 'bottom' in the North–South direction, going one down doubled in Six Hearts (the 'x' represents a doubled contract) and scoring minus 200 and 0 matchpoints.

As you see, overtricks are much more important in a Pairs event than in rubber bridge. If you make ten tricks in 3NT, you beat all the pairs who managed to score only nine tricks. You get two matchpoints for each pair that you beat, whether the margin is just 30 or several hundred. So, in a Pairs event you may sometimes put your contract at risk, searching for a valuable overtrick. It is an important part of this form of the game, to judge what risks are worth taking.

The pair with the highest total of matchpoints for all the boards will win the session. In some clubs the scoring will be completed soon after the play is over. (If you have had an awful session, you may hurry home saying, 'I won't wait for the results!'). In other clubs, the scoring may be done the next day and you can either phone the organizer to see how you did, or wait until the following week to look at the posted results sheet.

Why should I play duplicate bridge?

Playing duplicate bridge is the best way to improve your game. By comparing your results with the other pairs, you can tell whether you did well on a board or not. This is not so easy to judge in rubber bridge, where you can win a session merely because you happened to be dealt very good cards.

Most bridge clubs are registered with the national bridge organization of the country. They will award 'master points' to those who do well in each event (usually the top third or top quarter of the field). By collecting these over your lifetime you can attain various levels, such as Local Master, County Master, even perhaps the exalted title of Lifemaster or Grandmaster.

We have reached the end of the book and the time has come for me to wish you good luck in the game – whatever your ambitions may be!

Answers to Test yourself questions

Chapter 1

1

	♠ A 3 2	
	♥ 8 3	
	♦ J 7 3	
	♣ A K 9 6 4	
♠ 8		♠ 9 7 4
♥ Q J 10 7 5		♥ 9 6 4 2
♦ K 10 8 5 4		♦ Q 9
♣ J 7		♣ Q 10 8 3
	♠ K Q J 10 6 5	
	♥ A K	
	♦ A 6 2	
	♣ 5 2	

West	North	East	South
–	1♣	Pass	1♠
Pass	2♠	Pass	4NT
Pass	5♥	Pass	6♠
End			

West leads the ♥Q against your small slam in spades. How will you plan the play?

You have two losers in diamonds and must hope to establish dummy's clubs, in order to provide one or more discards. If your play in clubs is to cash the ace-king and then to ruff the third round, you will make the slam only when clubs break 3–3.

A better line allows you to succeed against a 4–2 club break. Win the heart lead and draw just one round of trumps with the king.

Now lead a club and duck in the dummy! You win the red-suit return and draw a second round of trumps with the queen. Leaving one trump out for the moment, you cross to the ♣A and ruff a club with the ♠J. The club suit is now established – dummy has ♣A-9 left and East holds the bare ♣Q. You return to dummy with the ♠A, drawing East's last trump, and play the two good clubs, throwing both of your diamond losers.

Do you see that it would be a mistake to draw a second round of trumps (with the ♠Q) before ducking a club? When East won the ducked club, he could return a third round of trumps. This would remove the entry to dummy before you had established the club suit.

2

```
                    ♠ A 6 2
                    ♥ A 10
                    ♦ A 10 8 6 3
                    ♣ 8 5 3
     ♠ J 8 7                        ♠ Q 10 9 3
     ♥ 6 4 2          N             ♥ 8 5
     ♦ J 5 2      W       E         ♦ K Q 7 4
     ♣ Q J 10 7       S             ♣ 9 6 4
                    ♠ K 5 4
                    ♥ K Q J 9 7 3
                    ♦ 9
                    ♣ A K 2
```

West	North	East	South
–	1♦	Pass	1♥
Pass	1NT	Pass	3♥
Pass	4♥	Pass	4NT
Pass	5♣	Pass	6♥
End			

South's 4NT is Roman Key-card Blackwood (see Chapter 2) and the 5♣ response shows three or zero aces. West leads the ♣Q against your small slam in hearts. How will you play the contract?

You need to set up dummy's diamond suit, so you can discard one of your black-suit losers. To achieve this, you will need to use both of dummy's entries in the trump suit. Win the club lead and play a diamond to the ace immediately. Ruff a diamond and return to dummy with the ♥10. When you ruff another diamond, you are pleased to see the suit break 4–3. You return to dummy with the ♥A and ruff yet another diamond, establishing a winner in the suit. You draw the last trump and cross to the ♠A. You can then discard a spade or a club on the thirteenth diamond, making your slam.

As it happens, a trump lead would beat the slam. It would remove an entry to the dummy prematurely, before you were able to make use of it.

Chapter 2

1 **a** 5♠. Two key cards and the queen of trumps.

   b 5♣. Three key cards.

   c 5♥. Two key cards without the queen of trumps.

2 **a** 6♣. 'I do hold the trump queen, also the ♣K.'

   b 6♥. 'I do not hold the trump queen.'

   c 5NT. 'I hold the trump queen but no side-suit king.'

3 **a** 6♣. You show the ♣K.

   b 6♠. With no side-suit king, you sign off in the trump suit.

   c 6♣. With two side-suit kings, you start by showing the lower king. If partner continues with 6♦, you will have the chance to bid 6♥, showing your other king.

Chapter 3

1

	♠ A Q J 2	
	♥ J 10 4 3	
	♦ Q 7 3	
	♣ 7 4	

West	North	East	South
–	–	–	1♥
2♦	3♥	Pass	4♥
End			

Your partner, West, cashes the ace and king of diamonds against South's heart game. He then continues with a third round of diamonds to dummy's queen. How should you defend?

You should ruff with the ♥8. South may or may not hold another diamond, but it cannot assist you to ruff with the ♥6 instead. Declarer has to overruff your ♥8 with the ♥K and your partner's ♥Q is promoted. That is three tricks for the defence and your ♠K will make it four. One down!

As you see, if you carelessly ruff with the ♥6, declarer will overruff with the ♥7 and draw trumps with the ♥A and ♥K, making the contract.

2

♠ 9 5 3 2
♥ A
♦ K Q 9 4
♣ J 5 3 2

♠ K 10 4   ♠ 7
♥ Q J 8 5 2   ♥ 10 9 6
♦ 6 5 3   ♦ J 10 8 2
♣ 9 6   ♣ A K 10 7 4

♠ A Q J 8 6
♥ K 7 4 3
♦ A 7
♣ Q 8

West	North	East	South
–	–	–	1♠
Pass	3♠	Pass	4♠
End			

Sitting West, you lead the ♣9 against South's spade game. East
wins with the ♣K and cashes the ♣A. He continues with a third
round of clubs and declarer ruffs with the ♠Q. How should you
defend?

If you overruff, with the ♠K, you will score just one trump trick
and the contract will be made. (Declarer will be able to draw your
last two trumps with the ♠A-J.) Discard, instead, and all your
trumps will move up one notch. You will score both the ♠K and
the ♠10 and the contract will go one down.

Chapter 4

1

```
                    ♠ K 5 2
                    ♥ A 6 4
                    ♦ A Q J 4
                    ♣ 8 5 4
    ♠ 6                           ♠ Q 8 4
    ♥ J 10 9 3      N             ♥ K Q 8 7 5
    ♦ 10 6 5 3   W     E          ♦ 8 2
    ♣ A Q 9 2      S              ♣ J 10 6
                    ♠ A J 10 9 7 3
                    ♥ 2
                    ♦ K 9 7
                    ♣ K 7 3
```

West	North	East	South
–	1♦	Pass	1♠
Pass	1NT	Pass	4♠
End			

West leads the ♥J against your spade game. You win and play the
♠K. If you continue with spade to the ace, West showing out, you
will go down. When you switch to diamonds, hoping to discard
one of your club losers in time, East will ruff the third round.
He will then switch to the ♣J, giving the defenders three tricks in
that suit.

To keep the dangerous East hand off lead, you should finesse the
♠J on the second round. As it happens, the finesse will win. You
will not lose a trump trick and can discard one of your clubs on the
fourth round of diamonds, ending with an overtrick.

The point of this play is that you will make the contract whether or
not the trump finesse wins. Suppose West wins the second round of
trumps from an original holding of ♠Q-6. He cannot attack clubs
effectively from his side of the table. He will probably play another
heart. You will ruff and play four rounds of diamonds, discarding

one of your club losers on the fourth round. The spade finesse on the second round is a win–win play that guarantees the contract.

2

♠ 2
♥ A 8 6 4
♦ A J 5 4
♣ A 9 5 4

♠ K 10 8 6 3
♥ J 10 9 3
♦ 6
♣ Q 10 2

♠ Q 9 5 4
♥ Q 7 5
♦ Q 9 2
♣ J 8 6

♠ A J 7
♥ K 2
♦ K 10 8 7 3
♣ K 7 3

West	North	East	South
–	–	–	1♦
Pass	1♥	Pass	1NT
Pass	3NT	End	

How will you play 3NT when West leads the ♠6 and East plays the ♠Q?

You should win with the ♠A, retaining the ♠J-7 as a partial stopper in the suit. You now need to develop nine tricks without allowing East (the danger hand, who can lead through your spade tenace) on lead. You have seven tricks on top and can easily develop two more from the diamond suit, even if you take a losing finesse there. You should cross to the ♦A and then finesse the ♦10.

When the cards lie as in the diagram, the finesse will win. Suppose it had lost to a doubleton queen with West, though. You would still make 3NT. You would have four diamond tricks, enough for the contract, and the safe hand would be on lead. West cannot profitably continue spades from his side of the table.

Chapter 5

1 a 2♦. Perfect for a weak two-bid. You have some solidity in the long suit and the four-card clubs will assist the playing strength.

   b 1♥. You should not open a weak 2♥ when you have such a strong four-card spade suit on the side. A pass is possible, but the hand is worth a one-bid.

   c Pass. In general, a pre-emptive bid should have good playing strength if trumps are chosen and little defence if the opponents choose trumps. Here the opposite is the case. The heart suit is very weak and there are two aces on the side. If you open such hands with a pre-empt, it is difficult for partner to judge what to do later in the bidding.

2 a 4♥. With four-card support and a reasonable six-card side suit, you do not expect to lose a big penalty in 4♥. At the same time there is every reason to expect that the opponents can make a big contract in one of the black suits. Make life difficult for them with a pre-emptive raise!

   b 2♠. There may well be a game available somewhere. Begin with a forcing bid in a new suit, hoping that partner can raise.

   c Pass. It is very unlikely that you can make game. Certainly you would not be justified in responding 2NT and advancing to game just because partner told you he was upper-range.

3 a 3♦. Lower-range with two top honours.

   b 3♠. Upper-range with two top honours.

   c 3♥. Upper-range without two top honours.

Chapter 6

1

```
              ♠ 8 5 3
              ♥ A 6 3
              ♦ A K 7
              ♣ 10 8 5 4
♠ J 10 9 4      ┌─────────┐      ♠ 7
♥ Q 10 8 2      │    N    │      ♥ J 9 5 4
♦ Q J 10 5      │  W   E  │      ♦ 9 6 4 2
♣ 2            │    S    │      ♣ K Q J 9
              └─────────┘
              ♠ A K Q 6 2
              ♥ K 7
              ♦ 8 3
              ♣ A 7 6 3
```

West	North	East	South
–	–	–	1♠
Pass	2♣	Pass	4♣
Pass	4♠	End	

West leads the ♦Q against your spade game. You win with the ♦A in dummy and draw two rounds of trumps, East discarding a diamond on the second round. How will you continue?

If clubs break 3–2, you can simply draw one more round of trumps and play ace and another club. You win the diamond return and set up a long card in clubs, still with control of the trump suit. You must next ask yourself whether there is a line of play that will succeed when the clubs break 4–1.

The best line of play is (how did you guess?) a dummy reversal. You have five winners in the side suits. If you can score all five trumps in the South hand, the total will come to ten whether or not the clubs break 3–2. You draw a third round of trumps, cash the ♣A and cross to the ♦K to ruff a diamond in your hand. You continue with king, ace and another heart, ruffing once again in the South hand. The contract is yours and, with the clubs 4–1, you could not have made the contract any other way.

2

♠ K J 9
♥ 8 6 3
♦ A 5 2
♣ A 8 5 2

♠ 8 7 5
♥ 7 4
♦ Q 10 8
♣ Q J 10 9 4

♠ 4 2
♥ J 10 9 5
♦ J 7 4 3
♣ K 6 3

♠ A Q 10 6 3
♥ A K Q 2
♦ K 9 6
♣ 7

West	North	East	South
–	1♣	Pass	1♠
Pass	1NT	Pass	3♥
Pass	3♠	Pass	4NT
Pass	5♣	Pass	6♠
End			

West leads the ♣Q against your small slam in spades. How will you play the contract?

You have six winners in the side suits. If you can score three club ruffs in the South hand, playing a dummy reversal, you will be able to add six trump tricks to your total.

You win the club lead in dummy and ruff a club with the ♠10. You return to dummy with the ♦A and ruff another club with the ♠Q. A trump to the nine allows you to ruff dummy's last club with the ♠A. You then lead your last trump to dummy's king and draw the last trump with the jack. Twelve tricks are yours.

Chapter 7

1

```
              ♠ A 10 7
              ♥ 7 6 4 3
              ♦ K J 5
              ♣ K 9 7
♠ 8 5 3 2        N          ♠ 6
♥ K J 8 2    W       E      ♥ A 10 5
♦ A 8 4          S          ♦ 10 9 7 6 3
♣ 6 4                       ♣ 10 8 5 2
              ♠ K Q J 9 4
              ♥ Q 9
              ♦ Q 2
              ♣ A Q J 3
```

West	North	East	South
–	–	–	1♠
Pass	3♠	Pass	4♠
End			

Sitting West, with four trumps in your hand, you embark on a forcing defence by leading the ♥2. East wins with the ♥A, you are pleased to see, and continues with the ♥10 covered by the ♥Q and your ♥K. When you play the ♥J, declarer ruffs and plays the ace and king of trumps, partner discarding a diamond on the second round. Declarer now leads the ♦2 from his hand. How will you defend?

When declarer leads towards a king-jack combination in dummy, it is often right to play a smooth low card when you hold the ace in the second seat. You hope that declarer will try the jack, losing to partner's queen, and you will score two tricks in the suit. Play low here, though, and declarer will make the contract! He will score five trump tricks: four club tricks and one diamond trick.

Your forcing defence is working well and you should persevere with it. Declarer has already been reduced to the same number of trumps that you hold. So, you should rise with the ♦A and play a fourth round of hearts, forcing South to ruff again. He will then hold only one trump in each hand, while you have two trumps. He cannot draw your trumps and when he plays on the club suit you will ruff the third round for one down.

2

	♠ 7 4 3	
	♥ 9 7 5	
	♦ A J 3	
	♣ Q 9 7 5	
♠ A K 8 6		♠ –
♥ K Q J 8 2		♥ A 10 6 3
♦ 10 9		♦ 8 7 6 4
♣ 6 4		♣ J 10 8 3 2
	♠ Q J 10 9 5 2	
	♥ 4	
	♦ K Q 5 2	
	♣ A K	

West	North	East	South
–	–	–	1♠
2♥	2♠	3♥	4♠
End			

You lead the ♥K, winning the first trick, and continue with a second round of hearts, ruffed by declarer. When he leads the queen of trumps, you win with the king and your partner discards a low club. You force declarer with another heart and he continues with the jack of trumps. What now?

If you win with the ♠A the contract will be made. A fourth round of hearts will be ineffective because declarer can ruff with dummy's last trump (in the short-trump hand). So, hold up the ace of trumps for one round.

Declarer cannot counter this defence. If he plays another trump, you will win with the ace and force his last trump with another heart. If, instead, he starts to play his winners in the minor suits, you will score a ruff with your ♠8.

Chapter 8

1 **a** Double. Perfect for a negative double. You are strong enough and have both the unbid suits.

    b 2♥. There is no need to make a take-out (negative) double since you have already found a heart fit. In any case, you are not quite strong enough.

    c Pass. Playing negative doubles, you have to pass initially with a hand worth a penalty double. If the next player passes, your partner is likely to re-open with a take-out double, which you will pass.

2 **a** Double. Perfect for a responsive double. You have enough to bid at this level and both the minor suits. If, instead, you held four spades you would make some bid in that suit, expecting there to be a 4–4 fit.

    b 3♠. You expect partner to hold four spades, since this is the 'other major suit'. A response of 2♠ would be an underbid, suggesting around 6–9 points. With these values you should issue a strong game invitation with a jump to 3♠.

    c Pass. You would like to make a penalty double, yes, but a double would be responsive (for take-out), so you do best to pass. If the next player passes too, your partner may well double a second time, again requesting a take-out. You will be happy to pass the double for penalties.

3 **a** Double. Just right for a competitive double.

    b 3♣. You are not strong enough for a competitive double and have already found a club fit. Give a single raise.

    c Pass. You would like to double for penalties, perhaps, but a double would be competitive. If partner has 3–1–3–6 shape and extra values, he may compete with a further take-out double, which you would pass.

Chapter 9

1

♠ K Q 7
♥ A 10 8 6 3
♦ J 7 3
♣ 6 4

♠ 10 6 5
♥ Q J 4
♦ K 9 6
♣ 10 9 8 2

♠ J 9 3 2
♥ –
♦ A 10 8 5
♣ Q J 7 5 3

♠ A 8 4
♥ K 9 7 5 2
♦ Q 6 2
♣ A K

West	North	East	South
–	–	–	1♥
Pass	4♥	End	

West leads the ♣10 against Four Hearts. You win and play the ♥K,
East showing out on the first round. You would like the defenders to
make the first play in diamonds. Play a trump to the ace, cash your
remaining club winner and continue with the three top spades. With
spades and clubs now eliminated, this position has been reached:

♠ –
♥ 10 8 6
♦ J 7 3
♣ –

♠ –
♥ Q
♦ K 9 6
♣ 9 8

♠ J
♥ –
♦ A 10 8 5
♣ Q

♠ –
♥ 9 7 5
♦ Q 6 2
♣ –

You now throw West on lead with the ♥Q. He will have to make the first play in diamonds or give you a ruff-and-discard.

2

```
              ♠ Q 10 8 3 2
              ♥ A 9 2
              ♦ 7 5 3
              ♣ K 4
♠ 4                              ♠ 6
♥ Q J 10 7 4    N                ♥ K 6 5 3
♦ K Q 8      W     E             ♦ 9 6 4 2
♣ J 9 5 2       S                ♣ Q 8 7 6
              ♠ A K J 9 7 5
              ♥ 8
              ♦ A J 10
              ♣ A 10 3
```

West	North	East	South
–	–	–	1♠
Pass	4♠	Pass	6♠
End			

You win the ♥Q lead with the ♥A, draw the defenders' trumps with the ♠Q and ruff a heart in your hand. You cash the king and ace of clubs and ruff a club (eliminating clubs). You ruff dummy's last heart (eliminating hearts) and return to dummy with the ♠10, leaving these cards still to be played:

```
              ♠ 8 3 2
              ♥ –
              ♦ 7 5 3
              ♣ –
♠ –                              ♠ –
♥ J 10          N                ♥ K
♦ K Q 8      W     E             ♦ 9 6 4 2
♣ J             S                ♣ Q
              ♠ A K J
              ♥ –
              ♦ A J 10
              ♣ –
```

You now lead a diamond to the jack. West wins and is end-played. He must return a diamond into your tenace or give you a ruff-and-discard.

Chapter 10

1 a 4♥. With a five-card fit, you jump to the four-level. This is what players call a 'two-way bid'. For all you know, partner may make the contract. The bid may also work well because it shuts out the player in the fourth seat. It is possible that North–South have a good spade fit, for example.

   b 2♥. With a three-card fit, you should not carry the bidding beyond the two-level unless you hold the high-card points to do so.

   c 3♦. Here you have a genuine high-card raise to the three-level. Since a direct raise to 3♥ would be pre-emptive, you must begin with a cue-bid.

2 a 3♣. With three-card support including a top honour, you are keen to raise the bidding one level. As well as removing bidding space from the opener, you tell partner that you would be happy for him to lead a club if the opponents win the auction.

   b 2♥. Here you have a sound high-card raise of partner's clubs. You indicate this with a cue-bid in the enemy suit.

   c 2NT. When your fit is in a minor suit, the most obvious target is 3NT rather than five of a minor. Here you have a very good stopper in the opponent's suit and it is more helpful to bid 2NT rather than to make a cue-bid in the enemy suit.

3 a 2♠. With a hand in the 8–10 point range you make a single jump in your preferred trump suit.

   b 2♥. Here you have a strong hand but no idea which denomination will be best. You begin with a cue-bid to show the strength of your hand.

c 2NT. With 11 points and a double stopper in the opponent's suit, your best bid is 2NT.

Chapter 11

```
              ♠ Q 5 4 2
              ♥ 9 7 2
              ♦ A Q 4
              ♣ K J 4
♠ A J                          ♠ 7
♥ K Q J 8          N           ♥ 10 6 4 3
♦ 9 8 6        W       E       ♦ 10 7 3 2
♣ Q 9 7 5          S           ♣ A 10 8 2
              ♠ K 10 9 8 6 3
              ♥ A 5
              ♦ K J 5
              ♣ 6 3
```

West	North	East	South
1NT	Pass	Pass	2♠
Pass	4♠	End	

West opens a 12–14 point 1NT and you end in 4♠. How will you play this contract when West leads the ♥K?

You win with the ♥A and turn your attention first to the trump suit. Since only West can possibly hold ♠A-J-6, you should lead the king on the first round of spades. West wins with the ♠A and East follows with the ♠6. When West continues with the queen and jack of hearts, you ruff the third round and draw West's last trump, the jack. You now need to guess the club suit in order to make the contract. What guess will you make?

West has shown up with 11 points in the major suits (five in spades and six in hearts). If he held the ♣A in addition, he would have a total of 15 points, which is too much for his weak 1NT opening.

You should therefore lead a club towards dummy and finesse the
♣J. When this forces East's ♣A, the contract is yours.

Suppose West had opened with a strong 1NT of 15–17 points
instead. He would then need the ♣A to bring his total to the
required 15 points. You would play a club to dummy's king
instead, again making the contract.

2

West	North	East	South
3♥	Pass	Pass	3♠
Pass	4♠	End	

West leads the ♥K, East overtaking with the ♥A and returning a
second round of hearts to the ten and jack. How will you play the
contract when West then switches to the ♣7?

West holds seven hearts to his partner's two, so it is quite likely
that East will hold more trumps than West does. You should
win the club switch with the ♣K and lead the ♠J from dummy,
planning to play East for ♠K-10-8-2, ♠K-10-8, ♠K-10-2 or
♠K-8-2.

Let's assume that East covers with the ♠K. You win with the ace
and re-enter dummy with the ♣Q to finesse the ♠9. Your card
reading proves to be valid and the finesse succeeds. You draw

East's last trump with the ace and must now guess the diamond suit. Will you lead low to the jack or low to the king?

Most players would rate ♥K-Q-J-x-x-x-x and the ♦A as too much for a three-level opening, so you should play West for the ♦Q. You lead a diamond to the jack and ... yes! It does force East's ace. The spade game is yours.

Chapter 12

1

	♠ A 7 6 4	
	♥ Q 7	
	♦ A K 5	
	♣ 9 8 7 2	
♠ Q 8 2		♠ J 10 5
♥ A 10 8 5 3		♥ 9 6 2
♦ 8 7 4		♦ J 10 6 3
♣ 6 4		♣ A K 3
	♠ K 9 3	
	♥ K J 4	
	♦ Q 9 2	
	♣ Q J 10 5	

West	North	East	South
–	–	–	1♣
Pass	1♠	Pass	1NT (12–14)
Pass	3NT	End	

Sitting West, you lead the ♥5 against 3NT. The ♥7 is played from dummy, covered by East's ♥9 and declarer's ♥K. Declarer crosses to dummy with the ♦A and leads the ♣2. East wins with the ♣K and returns the ♥6, South playing the ♥4. How will you defend from this point?

If East held the ♥J he would have played it at Trick 1, instead of the ♥9. So, declarer began with ♥K-J-4 (or possibly ♥K-J-4-2). You should allow the ♥K to win, retaining your ♥A as an entry. You expect East to hold the ♣A, because his ♣K won the first round of the suit. When East gains the lead with the ♣A you want him to have a heart to return.

When you duck the second round of hearts, declarer has no option but to play another club. East wins with the ♣A and returns the ♥2. You can now score three heart tricks to put the contract one down.

2

             ♠ Q J 7
             ♥ J 5
             ♦ A K Q J 5
             ♣ 7 5 2

♠ K 9 6 3   ♠ 8 5 2
♥ 8 6   N   ♥ A K 9 7 3 2
♦ 7 6 4   W   E   ♦ 8 2
♣ K 9 6 4   S   ♣ Q 8

             ♠ A 10 4
             ♥ Q 10 4
             ♦ 10 9 3
             ♣ A J 10 3

West	North	East	South
–	1♦	1♥	2NT
Pass	3NT	End	

Your partner, West, leads the ♥8 against 3NT and the ♥J is played from dummy. What is your plan for the defence?

Suppose you win dummy's ♥J with the ♥K. Whether you play the ♥A next or a low heart, the link with your partner will be broken. When declarer takes a losing spade finesse, seeking the extra trick that he needs, your partner will win with the ♠K but will have no heart to return. Declarer can win his switch and score an easy nine tricks.

To keep in touch with your partner, you must retain your two heart honours, allowing the ♥J to win. The best card to play is an encouraging ♥9. Declarer now has eight top tricks (one heart, five diamonds and two black aces). He will no doubt take the spade finesse. Unfortunately for him, West will win with the ♠K and return his remaining heart. You will enjoy five heart tricks, putting the game two down.

It's possible that your partner has only one heart, South holding ♥Q-10-6-4. In that case you and your partner cannot keep in touch however you defend and the contract will surely be made. When you need the cards to lie in a particular way to give you a chance of beating the contract (here you need West to hold two hearts), always assume that they do indeed lie that way. Some chance is better than none!

Chapter 13

1

	♠ K 9 7 3	
	♥ J 10 9 5	
	♦ A 9 7 4	
	♣ 7	
♠ J 6		♠ Q 10 8 2
♥ 8 6		♥ 7 3 2
♦ Q J 10 6		♦ K 8 5 2
♣ A Q 9 6 4		♣ K 8
	♠ A 5 4	
	♥ A K Q 4	
	♦ 3	
	♣ J 10 5 3 2	

West	North	East	South
–	–	–	1♣
Pass	1♦	Pass	1♥
Pass	3♥	Pass	4♥
End			

West leads the ♦Q against your game in hearts. How will you play the contract?

You win with dummy's ♦A and see that you have three winners in the side suits. If you can score seven trump tricks (one round of trumps and six trumps scored separately), this will bring your total to ten. Since you will need to ruff clubs in the dummy, the next move is to lead dummy's singleton club. Let's say that the defenders win and return a trump. What then?

You win with the ♥A and cash two rounds of spades, making sure of your tricks in the side suits before the defenders have any chance to discard spades. You then ruff a diamond with the ♥4. Your remaining five trumps (♥J-10-9 in the dummy and ♥K-Q in your hand) are all masters. You can therefore cross-ruff clubs and diamonds without fear of an overruff.

As on other deals in this chapter, a trump lead would have been effective, cutting down your potential ruffs. There was no pressing reason for West to lead a trump and most players would have led the ♦Q.

```
2                    ♠ 5
                     ♥ A K 2
                     ♦ K Q 9 5
                     ♣ A J 9 6 3

     ♠ K Q 9 6 2        ┌─────────┐        ♠ 10 4
     ♥ 10 9 8 6 4       │    N    │        ♥ 7 5
     ♦ 7               │ W     E │        ♦ 8 6 3 2
     ♣ 7 4             │    S    │        ♣ K Q 10 8 2
                        └─────────┘
                     ♠ A J 8 7 3
                     ♥ Q J 3
                     ♦ A J 10 4
                     ♣ 5
```

West	North	East	South
–	–	–	1♠
Pass	2♣	Pass	2♦
Pass	4NT	Pass	5♥
Pass	6♦	End	

West leads the ♥10. How will you plan the play?

A successful cross-ruff will give you eight trump tricks. If you can add four side-suit tricks, this will be enough for your small slam. So, the two black aces and just two heart tricks will suffice. You should therefore cash a second heart trick immediately, before one of the defenders (East on the lay-out shown) has a chance to discard his hearts.

With two heart tricks taken, you cash the black-suit aces and take your first two ruffs, one in each black suit, with low trumps. You can then take six more ruffs with master trumps, making the slam.

Do you see what would go wrong if you mistakenly attempted to cash three rounds of hearts? East would ruff the third heart and might then return a trump. You would then go down, no longer able to score the eight trump tricks that you need.

(Suppose you bid all the way to 7♦ instead. You would then need five winners in the side-suits to go with your eight trump tricks. You would have to risk cashing three rounds of hearts at the start of the play.)

Chapter 14

1   a   Respond 2♥ and pass 2♠. Even if partner breaks the transfer, rebidding 3♠, you should still pass.

   b   With 13 points, you should respond 2♦ and continue with 3NT on the next round to offer partner a choice of games. You are not strong enough to introduce the club suit because an 11-trick game will probably be too high on these values.

   c   Respond 2♥ and rebid 3♦, showing a strong hand with five spades and at least four diamonds.

2 **a** Begin with a Stayman 2♣. Unless partner responds 2♥, giving you a 4–4 heart fit, continue with 3♣.

     b With only 12 points, you are not strong enough to consider playing in 5♦. Use Stayman to discover if there is a 4–4 spade fit. If partner rebids 2♦ or 2♥, bid 3NT next. (The sequence 1NT – 2♣ – 2♥ – 3NT shows four spades, since otherwise you would have no reason to bid Stayman. Partner should therefore bid 4♠ with four cards in both majors.)

     c Your hand is strong enough to venture a game in hearts. Begin with a 2♦ transfer and rebid 4♥. By making partner the declarer you avoid a lead through his potential spade and diamond tenaces.

3 **a** Begin with a Stayman 3♣. Unless partner responds 3♥, when you will have a 4–4 heart fit, continue with 4♣ (natural and forcing).

     b With only 6 points, you are not strong enough to consider playing in 5♦. Begin with 3♥, to show five spades, and rebid 3NT to offer a choice of games.

     c You do not have enough for game, but 3♥ should be a better contract than 2NT. So, respond 3♦, intending to pass 3♥. If partner has a great heart fit, he may break the transfer, rebidding 4♥. In that case the game may well be made.

Chapter 15

1

	♠ A 9 6 2	
	♥ 2	
	♦ A K 7 5 3	
	♣ A Q 2	
♠ 8 3		♠ K 5
♥ Q 9 8 6 4		♥ J 10 5 3
♦ 8		♦ 10 9 6 4
♣ J 8 5 4 3		♣ 10 7 6
	♠ Q J 10 7 4	
	♥ A K 7	
	♦ Q J 2	
	♣ K 9	

West	North	East	South
–	1♦	Pass	1♠
Pass	4♠	Pass	4NT
Pass	5♣	Pass	6♠
End			

West leads the ♦8 against your small slam in spades. How will you plan the play?

If you had overbid to a contract of 7♠, you would make the 'normal' play in the spade suit, running the ♠Q. That's because you could not afford to lose a trump trick and finessing against the king is very much better than trying to drop a singleton king offside. Since you are in the more sensible contract of 6♠, you can afford a trump loser. What you cannot afford is to lose a diamond ruff as well. West's lead in dummy's main suit is very suspicious and the odds are high that the ♦8 is a singleton. What can you do about it?

The answer is that you should not take a trump finesse. Instead, you should play ace and another trump. East will take a trick with the ♠K, but since West has no trumps left the defenders cannot then score a diamond ruff. You don't mind at all if West began with ♠K-x or ♠K-x-x. He is welcome to score a trick with the ♠K because you cannot then lose a diamond ruff in addition. All that will be lost is a potential overtrick. It is worth giving up a few 30-point overtricks in order to make slams that would otherwise have gone down!

2

West	North	East	South
–	–	–	1NT (15–17)
Pass	3NT	All Pass	

West leads the ♠J against your contract of 3NT. You have eight top tricks and therefore need only one more trick from the diamond suit (a total of two diamond tricks) to give you the contract. In other words, you must look for a safety play for two diamond tricks. Can you see it?

After winning the first spade trick, in either hand, you should cash the ♦A and then duck a round of diamonds. When the cards lie as in the diagram, the ♦K will fall from East and you will have the two diamond tricks that you need. If the ♦K does not fall, you will win the defenders' return and lead towards the ♦Q on the third round, still making the contract when West holds the ♦K or the diamond suit breaks 3–3.

Suppose next you were in the same contract but dummy's clubs were only ♣10-5-2. With just seven top tricks now, you would need three diamond tricks to give you the game. You would therefore make the 'normal' play in diamonds, ace first and then low to the queen. When West held ♦K-x-x, you would score the required three diamond tricks and make the contract.

Chapter 16

1

```
                    ♠ Q
                    ♥ 8 5 2
                    ♦ Q J 10 7 3
                    ♣ 9 8 4 3
  ♠ 10 9 8 7 3          N          ♠ K 5 4 2
  ♥ A 7         W           E      ♥ Q 10 9 6
  ♦ 9 8 5                          ♦ A 6 4
  ♣ 10 7 2               S         ♣ 6 5
                    ♠ A J 6
                    ♥ K J 4 3
                    ♦ K 2
                    ♣ A K Q J
```

West	North	East	South
–	–	–	2NT
Pass	3NT	End	

West leads the ♠10 against 3NT and, sitting East, you cover dummy's ♠Q with the ♠K. Declarer wins with the ♠A and plays the ♦K, West signalling his count with the ♦5. Since declarer must hold at least two diamonds for his 2NT opening, it is clear that you should hold up your ♦A on the first round. At Trick 3, declarer continues with the ♦2, your partner playing the ♦8 and dummy playing the ♦Q. What now?

West has shown three diamonds by playing low–high in the suit. This leaves declarer with only two diamonds and you should therefore win the second round of the suit. You return a spade and declarer has no way to make the contract.

On this deal it was essential for you to take the ♦A at exactly the right moment. Suppose you had ducked the ace for a second time. Declarer would then have eight top tricks available and could have set up a ninth by leading a heart from dummy to his jack.

Next, suppose that the cards lie differently and your partner signals high–low in diamonds, playing the ♦8 followed by the ♦5. When partner holds two diamonds, declarer will hold three. So you would hold up the ♦A until the third round, restricting declarer to two diamond tricks instead of four.

2

	♠ A 6 2	
	♥ J 6	
	♦ Q J 10 8 6 3	
	♣ 8 5	

♠ J 10 7 4		♠ 9 8 3
♥ K Q 10 9 4	N	♥ 5 2
♦ 7 2	W E	♦ A K 4
♣ 9 7	S	♣ J 10 6 4 3

	♠ K Q 5	
	♥ A 8 7 3	
	♦ 9 5	
	♣ A K Q 2	

West	North	East	South
–	–	–	1♣
Pass	1♦	Pass	2NT
Pass	3NT	End	

West, your partner, leads the ♥K against 3NT. Declarer ducks the first trick and West continues with the ♥Q, which is also allowed to win. When West plays the ♥10, dummy discards a club and you throw a low spade. Declarer wins with the ♥A and leads the ♦9, West following with the ♦7. What is your plan for the defence?

If you win the first round of diamonds, declarer will win your black-suit return in the South hand and clear the diamond suit. The defenders will score just two hearts and two diamonds and declarer will make the contract.

To defeat 3NT you must hold up on the first round of diamonds, even though you hold two stoppers in the suit. The contract will then go one down. By holding up in this way, you restrict declarer to just one diamond trick.

Chapter 17

1 **a** 2NT. Perfect for an Unusual No-trump overcall. You have two sound suits, offering you every protection against a big penalty.

    b Double. With a flat 20-count, you start with a double. 2NT would show the minors, remember.

    c 2♥. Perfect for a Michaels cue-bid.

2 **a** 3♦. Partner has shown at least five cards in both minors. You choose diamonds because you have better support for diamonds than for clubs.

    b 3♣. You prefer clubs to diamonds. It is not your fault that you don't have better support.

    c 5♣. With such excellent club support, there is a good chance that you can make game.

3 **a** 4♠. Even if partner has quite a modest Michaels cue-bid, you should have a good play for game.

b 3♣. You want to play in partner's minor suit at the three-level. If partner holds spades and diamonds, he will bid 3♦ now.

c 2NT. Make the special relay bid to discover which minor suit partner holds. You can then raise to game in that suit.

Chapter 18

1

	♠ Q 5	
	♥ Q 9 6 2	
	♦ A Q 4	
	♣ A 7 4 2	
♠ A K J 10 7 6 3		♠ 9 8 2
♥ 7 4		♥ 8 5
♦ 8 6 3		♦ 10 9 7 2
♣ 5		♣ J 10 8 3
	♠ 4	
	♥ A K J 10 3	
	♦ K J 5	
	♣ K Q 9 6	

West	North	East	South
3♠	Pass	Pass	4♥
Pass	5♥	Pass	6♥
End			

North's 5♥ asked partner to bid a slam if he held a control (ace, king, singleton or void) in the enemy spade suit. How would you play the small slam when West leads the ♠K – East signalling count with the ♠2 – and continues with the ♠A?

You draw trumps in two rounds and all now depends on bringing in the club suit without loss. Whenever you have a potential key guess to make in a suit, it may help you to play the other side suits first. Your aim is to obtain a complete count of the hand. When you play three rounds of diamonds, important information comes to light. West follows all the way. That marks his shape as 7–2–3–1 (or possibly 7–2–4–0). Since West can hold at most one club, you cash the ♣A on the first round. Two lowly spot cards appear and you know, from your count of the hand, that East has ♣J-10-8 remaining. You lead a low club from dummy and, when East produces the ♣8, you finesse the ♣9. West shows out (surprise, surprise!) and the slam is yours.

It would do East no good to play the ♣J or ♣10 on the second round, of course, because you would win and return to dummy to finesse the ♣9 on the third round. Indeed, it would be poor defence for East to play one of his honours. By playing low instead, he would beat the slam whenever declarer had been too lazy to count the hand and was about to play the clubs from the top!

2

```
              ♠ Q 9 5
              ♥ Q J 6 2
              ♦ Q J 4
              ♣ A 10 4
  ♠ 8 7 4          N          ♠ J 10 6 2
  ♥ 10 9 8 5                  ♥ 7 3
  ♦ 10 9 6 2    W     E       ♦ A 7
  ♣ 7 5            S          ♣ Q 9 8 3 2
              ♠ A K 3
              ♥ A K 4
              ♦ K 8 5 3
              ♣ K J 6
```

West	North	East	South
–	–	–	2NT
Pass	4NT	Pass	6NT
End			

North's 4NT is a non-forcing limit bid that invites a slam. You decide to bid 6NT and West leads the ♥10, which you win with the ♥A. How will you play the contract?

Once you have forced out the ♦A you will have 11 top tricks. Unless you can score three diamond tricks, you will need to guess which defender holds the ♣Q. What is the best way to play the diamonds?

If the diamond suit breaks 3–3, all will be easy. You should lead twice towards dummy's ♦Q-J-4, which will also allow you to score three diamond tricks when West has a doubleton ♦A. As it happens, East wins the ♦Q with the ♦A and returns a heart. When you test the diamond suit, East discards a club on the third round. You now need to guess the club suit correctly. The defender who began with the majority of clubs will be favourite to hold the missing ♣Q and you must therefore play the other suits, aiming to build up a count on the hand.

Both defenders follow to three rounds of spades and when you play dummy's last two heart winners, East shows out on the third round and discards one spade and another club. You have a complete count on the hand. East began with 4–2–2–5 shape. The odds are therefore '5-to-2 on' that East was dealt the ♣Q. You cash dummy's ♣A and, at Trick 12, finesse the ♣J. Justice is served on this occasion. The finesse succeeds and the slam is yours.

Index

Image credits

Front cover: © Mike Kemp/Rubberball/Photolibrary.com

Notes

Notes

Notes

Notes